BONE OF CONTENTION

Life Story and Confessions

Frontispiece. As I look today – in my ninetieth year.

BONE OF CONTENTION

Life Story and Confessions

by

CYRIL SCOTT

ARCO PUBLISHING COMPANY, INC.

NEW YORK

Published 1969 by ARCO PUBLISHING COMPANY, INC.
219 Park Avenue South, New York, N.Y. 10003

© CYRIL SCOTT 1969

All Rights Reserved
Library of Congress Catalog Number 75-101239
Standard Book Number 668-02172-1

PRINTED IN GREAT BRITAIN

To

Marjorie,

without whose encouragement
I might have lacked the will
to complete this self-revealing book.

Preface

BERNARD SHAW made the extravagant statement that all autobiographies are lies, not unconscious, unintentional lies, but
deliberate ones. Yet surely it would be more veracious to say
that autobiographies are not all truths; by which I do not mean
that scrupulous autobiographers actually tell falsehoods about
facts, but simply omit those relating to their friends or themselves about which it would not be seemly or in good taste to
tell the truth. And this is the policy I have adopted in my own
confessions. I have even been obliged at their own request to
refer to some of my acquaintances by initials only, and in a few
cases, so as not to cause embarrassment to surviving relatives,
have thought it wise slightly to alter names.

I wish to stress here that any allusions to the B.B.C. have
been made in no hostile spirit. Having been born many years
before wireless was even dreamt of, I do not just accept it in the
light way that do many of those not old enough ever to have
known what it was to be without the amazing richness and
variety of entertainment it provides, and for which I for one
remain grateful, whatever its policy towards myself may be.
Not thinking I would ever come to write my complete life story,
I have kept very few letters to help me in the matter of actual
dates. Yet after all, are dates of much importance except in
history books?

Contents

A*

List of Illustrations

Frontispiece, 9*a*, 9*b* and 10. Photographs by
Maurice Manssen.

CHAPTER I

Introducing Myself

A<small>UTOBIOGRAPHIES</small>, in particular those well interlarded with confessions, have not been written in vain if they contribute to a better understanding of human nature. But if in addition they incidentally draw attention, as some of them do, to subjects which the more open-minded of their readers may be tempted to explore, then that is all to the good. Holding the belief that the more subjects one can, within limits, become interested in, the less time and inclination one has to be unhappy, I will make no excuses for what the friends of my music call my versatility, and its detractors the dissipation of my energies: for whichever way regarded I venture to hope that indirectly it may add interest to my own *confessions*.

In a sad plight is the composer who has no sideline or pastime to turn to during those desolate periods when musical ideation gives out, leaving but that painful sense of emptiness and frustration so familiar to all creative artists. But although the desolate periods themselves cannot be avoided, at least the misery of them is avoidable. My own method was to turn my attention *pro tem* away from music altogether and to go exploring in other fields of culture. That one of the subjects in which I became especially interested was closely connected with music, I only came to know in middle life.

I began my exploring when still a very young man, and now being an old one, in the long interim was my curious musical career, and concurrently my hobby, that of writing books by way of a rest in the form of a change of work. As some of those books deal with the occult or esoteric, it came to be said by certain of my detractors that had I not busied myself with such matters, I might have been a better composer! Yet as Professor

Norman Demuth pointed out in his *Musical Trends of the 20th Century*, it so happened that I was only drawn to those subjects *after* I had already established myself as a composer, and my music – such as it then was – had already become a 'bone of contention' . . . And perhaps not surprisingly so; for whilst the musical 'young bloods' of the day accepted with a certain schoolboyish glee my flouting of the academic conventions, as they then were, the professors and staider music lovers were loud in their denunciation of me. Since those days, however, the tonal conventions having so materially changed as to have gone to the opposite extremes, I am censured by the 'extremists' for not being a fellow 'extremist' and for not having 'progressed with the times', or conversely I am commended for not having been swayed by the prevailing tonal fashions, and thus for flouting the conventions as they now are. But then – to make my first confession – I do not believe that any composer who is influenced by the desire to be 'up-to-date' will ever write music possessing that so difficult-to-define quality which gives it its inherent and lasting appeal. And my belief is based on the fact that those composers of the past whose works have *lived*, were those who progressed, not with the times (in the sense that that phrase is bandied about) but along the lines of their own respective individualities and idioms.

As for Occultism, so as to correct misconceptions, it were well to point out the following: Occultism is the synthesis of Science, Philosophy and the esoteric aspects of Religions. In its highest and most comprehensive form it is that branch of knowledge pertaining to the subtler manifestations of Nature.* It was his study of Occultism which inspired Gustav Holst's splendid work *The Planets*, as also Scriabin's finest orchestral works. Incidentally, the late Sir Montague Norman, for twenty-five years Governor of the Bank of England, was a convinced occultist.

* See APPENDIX I.

CHAPTER II

Birth and Parents

THE era in which I was born (on September 27, 1879) had at least in its favour that it did possess a certain degree of refinement and dignity as well as being free from those noisome concomitants of our present mechanised epoch, which despite its increased material benefits, wonderful discoveries, inventions and exploits must still be accounted in many respects a vulgar and blatant age.

Not that I remember my native town of Birkenhead as being a strikingly refined one, though parts of it were pleasant enough. But at any rate when I was old enough to urge my unrobust body along even some of its ugliest streets I was not nearly poisoned by petrol fumes but only got whiffs of the rural odour of horse-dung in my nostrils, nor was I deafened by the roar of careering motor-cyclists and the discordant honks of motor-buses and similar vehicles, my world of sound being largely confined to the clip-clop of horses, the shouts of errand boys and newspaper sellers, with an occasional barrel-organ's music by way of contrast. Moreover, at nights my sleep was not disturbed by the 'thunder' of aeroplanes, which is more than can be said for many unfortunate people today . . . Incidentally, those cynics who are wont to sneer at the Victorian age because of its prudery, priggishness and hypocrisy might do otherwise if they had lived long enough to remember some of its good points.

Actually I drew my first breath and passed my infancy at Oxton, where my parents lived in a smallish house on the verge of the (then) country some few miles from the centre of Birkenhead. Strange to say it was named *The Laurels*, as if symbolic of the laurels I was subsequently to win and later on to lose. I have, however, no recollection of that house at all, for soon after my arrival on the scene, my father, Henry Scott, built a larger one in the same locality. Why certain persons should refer to this new house as having been 'built' by my father, struck my innocent mind as miraculously peculiar until the matter was explained to me as merely a manner of speaking, whereafter my father did not appear to me as 'quite the Hercules' I had imagined. At the time of my birth he was thirty-five, and my mother, Mary Scott, *née* Griffiths, was virtually the same age; and I consider myself lucky in having had parents who had reached their years of discretion before bringing me into the world. In some astrological books I read that it is characteristic of souls born with 'Sun in Libra' to all but die of pneumonia in their infancy, and then – unless they actually do die of it – to live to a good old age, when in many cases they finally pass out from a stroke. The books were written before the present methods of treating pneumonia; but anyhow my own birth date does give me 'Sun in Libra', and I did nearly die of pneumonia in infancy and have also contrived to live to a good old age. Whether I shall further give weight to astrological pronouncements by dying from a stroke remains to be seen.

Of my ancestors I know very little, except that part of the family hailed from the Potteries (Staffordshire), my paternal grandmother having originally been a Miss Meir. Hence I was christened Cyril Meir Scott – a matter which led some German people erroneously to assume that I had Jewish blood in my veins, for they chose to pronounce it Myer! Among my possessions, by the way, is the engraving of a wassail cup designed and made *circa* 1580 by one of my progenitors, Richard Meir of Burslem. I also possess a seal with the family crest, that of a boar's head with straw in its mouth, and underneath, the motto, *Do right, and let them say*. But how far I have contrived to carry out that wise injunction is of course a debatable point. Musically, as already implied, I have done what at least I *thought* to be right, and have been indifferent to criticism, whilst philosophically (if that is the correct word) I have never made a secret of my beliefs, not caring whether I was called a crank or anything else disapproving persons thought applicable.

My father – born 1843 not far from Wolverhampton – had adopted a business career connected with shipping. But, unlike most business men, as long as he had enough means to meet his liabilities he was never really interested in making money, his chief interest in life being Greek. He was, in fact, a Greek scholar and an authority on biblical Greek in particular. Prominence is given to his name in the third edition of Dr. Robertson's *Grammar of the Greek New Testament*, whilst tribute is paid to him by the late Dr. J. H. Moulton in the second edition of his *Prolegomena*. Nevertheless, he was so modest about his achievements and scholarship that he never thought to draw our attention to his name in these books, and neither my sister nor I knew anything about the matter till after his death. Altogether he was strangely secretive about his hobby, for although he would work at it for some two hours every morning before breakfast and again in the evening after business hours, not even his own brothers knew the precise nature of his studies until an obituary article in *The Expository Times* threw some light on the subject.

As regards his exterior he was of medium height, broad-shouldered and well built, had dark hair at the sides of his head but was bald on top, a high forehead, a thin and refined nose and a short, sandy unpointed beard. Being near-sighted he wore gold-rimmed spectacles. The general impression he gave was that of a healthy-looking scholar. Unlike his son, he was a man entirely without vices; he never drank alcohol, never smoked, and never even took tea or coffee by way of more or less harmless stimulants. He believed that the secret of good health was frugality and plenty of unviolent exercise. Thus, every morning, Sundays excepted, he walked the two-and-a-half miles through the dreary streets of Birkenhead down to the Ferry, took the boat across the Mersey to Liverpool, and then repeated the same performance in reverse order in the evening. Save for an occasional cold, he was never ill, that is, not until around his seventy-third year, when he developed the heart trouble which brought about his death at seventy-five.

His tastes, if limited, were essentially refined. In addition to his one absorbing hobby he loved good literature, especially good poetry, and above all, the beauties of Nature. He was totally unmusical, could with few exceptions hardly distinguish one tune from another, and for him the most beautiful music was the song of the birds. Thus one thing is obvious; I could not have inherited my musical inclinations from my father, although apart from literary tastes, I think and hope he did bequeath me some of his sense of humour. I wish I could add that he bequeathed me a few more of his other admirable qualities – but this would be to indulge in self-flattery.

My mother was in many respects the complement of her husband, and it might perhaps be said that she brought those elements into my make-up which in the nature of things he could not provide. Having Welsh blood in her veins – her name had been Mary Griffiths – she possessed that fondness for music, of a sort, which is characteristic of her race. Before her marriage she had played the piano with a certain superficial brilliance, and had even written a waltz, which somehow got into print. Admittedly her taste was far from highbrow, for she owned to preferring 'pieces with plenty of runs'. She had a voice of some volume and sweetness, but during my childhood could never exercise it when I was within earshot; for like Chopin had done when hearing *his* mother sing, I would immediately burst into tears.

In appearance she was moderately tall, neither stout nor thin but displaying that happy medium which is usually called a good figure. Judging from photographs, she had been a beautiful girl, and even when I had reached my teens, she was still a handsome woman. Although she suffered nearly all her married life from poor health, she did not look delicate, and carried herself erect until her late sixties. She died of bronchial pneumonia at the age of seventy-nine, having outlived my robust father by three years.

It is a distressing thing to have an ailing mother, and yet I doubt whether, had she been otherwise, she could have shown so much understanding towards my own sufferings when I was still a child. Indeed, by nature she was so tender-hearted (which is not to say that she pampered me) that she would weep in sympathy with nearly all afflicted persons who confided to her their sorrows. Much of her kind and sympathetic disposition being reflected in her face, she found favour in the sight of most of the people she met. Unlike her son, she had that useful faculty of being able to say in a pleasing and affable manner something about nothing – if the paradox be pardoned. Besides, her continuous efforts for charities made her popular, for she was forever crocheting shawls, dolls' clothes and what not for poor people, poor children, charity bazaars and the like.

As regards her attitude to life, she was not only a devout Christian but a really *good* woman – a by no means invariable combination. True, not being a scholar like my father, her religious outlook was narrow and Victorian, but that was to be expected in those days when God was supposed to be exceedingly particular as to how He was worshipped. Evidently my mother imagined that the Low Church method was the most pleasing to Him, from the services of which she obviously derived great comfort and spiritual satisfaction. What she did not realise in company with thousands of other sectarians was that, had she been brought up, say, in a Catholic family, she would then have believed the R.C. method to be the most acceptable to God; for what most people believe has little to do with Truth but much to do with upbringing. (Incidentally, who shall say what *is* Truth, since with our finite minds we can only gauge certain minute aspects of It?) In any case, her sectarian outlook did not adversely affect her amiable, kind, generous and sympathetic character; and if her conventionality – for she was conventional – came to cause me much annoyance in my early manhood, it was in part my own fault for not being more tolerant towards it.

Nevertheless, despite the fact that I was blessed with two admirable parents and was brought up in an atmosphere of domestic harmony, I was fated, because of my peculiar and sensitive temperament, to experience both physically and emotionally a most unhappy childhood.

CHAPTER III

Childhood

I was the third and last child in the Scott family. Prior to my arrival there was my sister, christened Mabel Louise, and a male child who had died in infancy. It would seem that bringing me into the world had overtaxed my mother's strength, for I was told that the doctor had said: 'Now that is enough, Mrs. Scott. No more!'

I nearly died in infancy myself – from pneumonia – but somehow managed to pull through and live to be a problem and a ceaseless anxiety to my parents. From an astrological point of view this is not without significance, seeing that in my horoscope I have Virgo rising, and many souls with this sign *nearly* die in infancy and then live to a ripe old age. This sign, with Sun in Libra, gives me my interest in diet and therapeutics; a matter which sneerers at astrology may think very strange in a musician.

My mother told me that I could play the piano before I could talk. Indeed, I was always clamouring to be lifted on to the piano stool, after which I would play by ear till exhausted. My greatest delights (subsequently to become my bugbear) were barrel-organs, the tunes of which I used to pick up and then play on the piano, even with harmonies that were not just discords. This feat seems to have caused some astonishment among my parents' acquaintances, and one dear old lady was moved to say: 'Now mark my words! That child will be a great musician!' Not that I myself can remember the incident, my mother having related it to me when reminiscing about my childhood. Nor can I remember when I was first taken to church; I only know from hearsay that the experiment was a complete fiasco, for no sooner did I hear the organ than I burst into loud lamentations and had to be taken home speedily, the experience being 'too much for my feelings'. So also was even my mother's hymn-tune playing, and the time came when, out of consideration for me, she had to refrain from giving musical expression to her religious enthusiasm whenever I was in the house.

These painful emotions persisted even beyond my actual childhood, and I attribute them partly to the fact that, having been told at a too early age that all living things had sooner or later to die, my mother's singing and hymn-tune playing aroused in me the sad thought that one day she would sing no more on earth, but only far away somewhere out of sight in heaven! (One must remember that I was born into an age of sentiment, bathos and morbidity, when people advertised their sorrows by wearing deep mourning, widows' weeds, and similar emblems of abysmal gloom.) Moreover, so obsessed did I become with the idea of death – not for myself but for others – that silently every night I prayed: "Please God may we all die together!" – though later on this petition was altered to: "Please God, may my parents live till I am forty!" Why I specified forty in particular was that I imagined by then I would be able to sustain their loss with fortitude. As it turned out, I did lose my father at forty and my mother some two years later.

I forget how long it was before I could endure the church organ without bursting into tears. In any event, once that embarrassing manifestation of my emotional nature had been overcome, my mother had the satisfaction of taking both her children to service every Sunday (when I was well enough) and of believing that the foundations of our religious education were thus being ensured. But unfortunately, the sort of religion I was taught only added to my troubles, for, miserable child that I already was, so much harping on death and the Christian hereafter only served to increase my melancholy. Further, I was tormented by the notion that should I suddenly die before I had had time to ask God to forgive some of my acts of naughtiness, I would then go to a frightful place called Hell, where I should burn for an eternity. Not that my father believed this appalling nightmare-tale, nor did my mother ever put it into so many words, but somehow that was the creed which got imprinted on my young mind.

Still, though I had much to suffer, my church-going gave me a certain familiarity with the Bible and its texts, which was to prove useful when years later I came to write some of my books; and above all, it was responsible for the beginnings of my musical education, for it was only in church that I heard any *good* music. In fact, the first time I ever heard fragments of Handel, Bach and Mendelssohn was on the organ in Christ Church, Claughton, where the Rev. Canon H. F. Robson officiated, and around which a great part of my mother's life tended to resolve.

Life at *The Laurels* seemed to be pervaded by an atmosphere of parsons. There was a large, framed photograph of Canon Robson, presented by himself, hanging in the drawing-room, and a smaller one reposing on the piano, to remind us all presumably that he was our spiritual shepherd and we were the sheep of his flock.

'The Canon', as he was referred to with distinctive abbreviation, looked the typical, full-figured, clean-shaven Church-Dignitary to perfection, was convinced that every word in the Bible was God-inspired, that the world had been created in (literally) six days, and that any cleric who thought otherwise had no right to preach the Christian religion. He was a widower having lost two wives; and at the time he christened me, possessed eleven children, some still small and others grown-up. He did not marry again, but, as one of his sons informed me, had always remained 'very fond of the ladies'. He wrote out every one of his sermons and then read them in the pulpit, but with eloquence. They never lasted less than twenty-five minutes, and when it was suggested that they were too lengthy and that he should shorten the time-limit, he indignantly replied that he 'would rather resign than do such a thing'. I doubt not that he was a thoroughly good and upright man; yet he was partly

responsible for implanting in my young mind a distaste for the
Church, which I came to associate with a certain pomposity
and unctuousness incompatible with the character and teachings of Jesus Christ as portrayed in the Gospels. After all, Jesus
led the life of a wandering *sannyasi*, with no fixed abode wherein
'to lay his head'; and although the Church, with all her pomp
and circumstance, her prelates and palaces, may have served a
given purpose (and we hope may still do so), yet it certainly
cannot be said that she is founded on the example of Christ.
But this is not to say that cathedrals, old churches, monks and
nuns and incense make no poetic appeal to me; on the contrary,
I went through a phase around my twenties when I imagined
that these outward signs of religion had an inspiring effect on
my musical activities.

It would be doing my mother an injustice if I suggested that
she was one of those women who think they are worshipping
God when all the time they are merely worshipping the cleric
who preaches to them *about* God. Even so, there is little doubt
that, like many others of her sex, she had a weakness for 'the
Cloth' and believed that parsons were something in the nature
of superior beings who helped one up the ladder from earth to
heaven. Most of these beings who frequented our house were
curates, and one in particular I recall because he seldom came
without bringing me something to cheer up my melancholy
spirit. He was not awe-inspiring like 'The Canon', and being
nervous and sensitive himself by temperament (for instance he
was afraid to travel by express trains) he comfortingly brought
home to my limited intelligence that it was not only children
who suffered from harassing emotions. As for some of the other
curates who lunched, dined or took tea at *The Laurels*, several of
them were so absurdly affected, that even mother had often to
repress a smile or make some feeble joke so that we could relieve
our risible urgings!

I may add that in relating all this I might similarly be relating the experiences of scores of other Victorian little boys who
were born of church-going parents, and whom friendly curates

petted, amused and cheered up – especially if the boys had good-looking mothers. But then, where autobiography is concerned, one cannot just alter facts to make one's life story more unusual and hence more entertaining for the reader.

CHAPTER IV

My painful Idiosyncrasies

U NLIKE *The Laurels* No. 1, where I was born, and which was perched on a hill commanding a view of the distant Welsh Hills, *The Laurels* No. 2 was an unromantic house built of yellow bricks and surmounted by a roof of red tiles. I always thought it an ugly house, but at least it was commodious and comfortable and surrounded by a fairly large garden, though not of a very picturesque type, for there was a certain Victorian artificiality about its orderliness.

In these surroundings I spent the greater part of my unhappy existence until I was twelve; unhappy through no fault of my wise and understanding parents, but because of my very poor health and inner sensitivity. I would in fact be tempted to gloss over this period as one that needs no detailed description if only I were certain that the children of today materially differed from those of my own childhood days.

Let me begin by saying that those people who declare that childhood is the happiest time of life, are either talking nonsense or have short memories. Indeed, the sorrows of children, I suggest, are just as real while they last as those of an adult, perhaps even more so, for they have no philosophy which helps them to bear them with fortitude. Children, among other unpleasant experiences, are constantly faced with frustration. At moments when a child may be thoroughly enjoying himself, along comes an elder who says he must be taken for a walk, must now go to bed, or do this, that and the other for which he (or she) has not the least inclination. All this of course is necessary discipline – for as well as truthfulness, every child should be taught obedience – but it is none the less a discipline he is too young to understand, and so he is unhappy. Moreover, a sensitive child is harassed by countless fears; fear of being scolded, fear of the dark, of thunder, of accidents to himself or his parents, of dogs, of burglars, of being murdered and other unlikely possibilities. All these fears I was destined to suffer during my childhood. In addition I was terrified of all lame men, an evil-tongued domestic having created this fear in me. There was a period lasting for months when I could not be induced to go out of the garden in case I might meet a lame man. My trouble was that I had too much imagination of the wrong kind. When, for instance, my mother went out shopping or visiting friends, I imagined something untoward might happen to her and she would never come back. Such fears, of course, appear ridiculous to an adult, but they were very real to my imaginative self.

I seem to have been an effeminate child, for I preferred to play with dolls rather than with tin soldiers. One day I thought I would like to be a hairdresser, and started by cutting the hair off my sister's latest doll! My parents were secretly amused, but none-the-less reprimanded me for this mutilation of another person's property.

Even in my earliest years, music (of a sort) was my chief delight, and when on one occasion I was given some money to buy my sister a birthday present, I bought her a drum, which she did not want at all, but I did, and being a selfish little boy, that was all I thought about.

Those were the days when I loved barrel-organs, and one of my childish games was to attach a piece of string to the back of a chair, wiggle it round like the handle of a barrel-organ, the while I would hum tunes. Then I would bring the chair to another part of the nursery and start the performance all over again! My ambition was to become an organ-grinder, preferably with a monkey. My parents used good-naturedly to tease me about this, as also about the drum incident, of which it was a long time before I heard the last.

Of sorrows, many were connected with the domestics. I used to become deeply attached to the nicer of them, and then when for one reason or another they left, I was harrowed unendurably. These heart-lacerations were all too frequent occurrences, not because my mother was an exacting mistress – quite the reverse – but because the domestics were so contentious that for days on end they refused to speak to each other. As the house was not a Trappist monastery and could not be run without the natural means of communication, the domestics concerned had to be given notice. Others had to leave because, despite an alarum clock, they were still asleep when they should have been lighting the fires. In consequence I, who suffered tortures from the cold during the winter months, had often to come down to an icy cold room for breakfast. I think the rest of the family suffered less because they were blessed with better circulations. Although my father was a laudably even-tempered man, one thing he could not tolerate was unpunctuality, since every morning he had to leave the house precisely at eight-thirty so as to catch the ferry boat to Liverpool. And so, over-sleeping and unpunctual servants had to go. I do not think we ever had any domestics who got drunk, but I did notice that one elderly cook who was especially kind to me had a somewhat alcoholic breath.

As children go, I was a moderately good one, not from any exalted motive, but simply because I was too much of a weakling to be otherwise. Not only did I hate being scolded myself, but would burst into tears if any other child was scolded in my presence, for any manifestation of anger upset me considerably.

Of all my afflictions the worst were the long and frequent fits of melancholy which in adults would be called deep depression. Much of this I now believe was due to my continuous state of ill-health resulting largely from the sort of diet both children and adults lived on in those days – many of them still do – and therefore I do not ascribe it entirely to the so-called artistic temperament. Even so, the most rational diet cannot cure a sensitive nature, but only make it more bearable. Nor in the case of creative artists is it desirable that it should, since poets, musicians and the like are gifted with certain mediumistic faculties for which sensitivity is indispensable – at least so I have good reasons for believing, which will become apparent anon.

CHAPTER V

Music Lessons and Others

WITH few exceptions I am not fond of children (I prefer
cats) and especially not the sort of child I was myself.
How anybody could have liked me is a mystery – though perhaps they didn't and only feigned to do so. In appearance I
was one of those very pale-haired and pale-faced little boys of
such meagre build that when washing me, my mother used to
say 'Why! you're as thin as a lath'. Fortunately for her she
did not have to contend with *two* sickly children, for my sister,
despite the deficiency-diet, was a normal, healthy, rosy-cheeked
little girl, quite untroubled with fears, sorrows or, for that
matter, any special talents. The latter circumstance my mother
regarded as a blessing, a frequently made remark of hers being
'One genius in the family is quite enough!' – this being her
semi-humorous reply when conversation-making acquaintances
asked: 'And is your little daughter also musical?'

I was usually dressed in a velvet or sailor suit, neither of
which I particularly liked. But at any rate as top garments
they caused me no physical sufferings, which is more than
could be said for the under-ones I had to wear, my skin being
so sensitive that they scratched and irritated it beyond en-
durance and caused me to shed many tears. And yet they were
the sort of things that most children wore in those days without
apparently being moved to rebellion. How I envied my sister
who was allowed to wear linen next to her skin, even though
she had layers of other garments under her dress, the names of
which, in those days, not being proper to mention, I soon
added to my limited vocabulary.

We children were blessed in our early years with a competent
and very devoted nursery governess. Her name was Maggie

28

Walker, and gratefully I pay tribute to her memory. She was so entirely to be trusted that my parents could send us away on holiday with her and be sure that we were in safe keeping. She even saved our lives on one occasion when near Hoylake at the mouth of The Dee, we got overtaken by the tide and had she not waded into deep water and rescued us, we should undoubtedly have been drowned. She did not live with us in *The Laurels* but came every morning after breakfast and stayed until we had been banished to bed in the evening.

Maggie Walker was not of the servant class and hence spoke grammatical English, albeit with a Cheshire accent. Her father had died leaving very little money, and she and her two elder sisters, with an old mother to keep, had been faced with finding some lucrative occupation.

It was one of her elder sisters who first taught me my notes, but unfortunately not how to use my fingers in the right way on the piano, for though I could play by ear and improvise fluently, I had merely formed bad 'digital habits' which should have been corrected before they became any worse. She also gave me and my sister our first schoolroom lessons in company with two little girls, one of them a mischievous red-haired little monkey who became my first female playmate. The tuition, however, after several months came to an untimely end, for one day our good preceptress was taken ill and shortly afterwards departed to more agreeable planes.

Our next preceptress was a Miss Kelly, whose brother Talbot Kelly acquired a reputation for painting pictures of Egypt. She had what in those days was called 'a sweet face', and it was not long before I found myself regarding her with feelings of a sentimental nature. In the summer months, weather permitting, our lessons took place in her garden, which would have been very pleasant had it not been in the vicinity of stables, from which a disagreeable odour floated whenever the wind was in a certain direction. It is said that a person with a good intellect is apt to have a highly perceptive nose. Yet though I was entirely destitute of the former, I was and have always been troubled by the more unpleasant aspects of the latter; indeed some of my associates say that I appear to be conscious of smells which don't exist. Be that as it may, thinking back along the years I cannot help associating the 'sweet face' of Miss Kelly with the less sweet odour of stables.

For how long it was that Miss Kelly struggled with our unretentive and inelastic minds I cannot remember, but I do remember that there was something slightly comic connected with her subsequent marriage, in that having started as a Miss Kelly she ended as a Mrs. Kelk.

Meanwhile music had never ceased to be the one absorbing interest in my life, and as soon as I had acquired the most elementary knowledge of notation I began to 'compose'. But it was a laborious business; having no manuscript paper I had to rule my own lines, on and between which I would make big 'potato notes' in pencil, the use of pen and ink not being allowed except under supervision.

I can still vaguely remember the first composition, which might best be described as 'exceedingly bad Chopin'. This may seem curious, for whereas I had been able to hear in church some Bach, Handel and fragments of other appropriate composers, not so of the illustrious Pole, whose music, apart from the *Funeral March*, would hardly have been considered suitable for the House of God. Still, the matter is of no importance. What *was* of importance, though I did not then realise it, was the correct training of my fingers; and, alas, that training I did not receive, but only a new teacher.

To say that Miss B. was a dishonest young woman would be to give a wrong impression, but she was a dishonest teacher, albeit a good musician. She had studied to her advantage with a long-and-greasy-haired German professor in Liverpool, from whom she had acquired a good technique and tone, neither of which qualities she conveyed to me, nor to my sister, whom she also taught. Had she been honest she would, after first hearing my showy efforts, have gone straight to my mother and said: 'The first thing I shall have to do is to put your little boy on five-finger exercises for at least three months, during which time he must not be allowed to touch the piano except to practise them. This is the only way of strengthening his fingers and of overcoming his bad habits'. But not a word of the kind did she say. All that concerned her apparently was to let me continue to make a show of playing well, when all the time she knew I was playing badly and along such lines never would play better. And with it all she was by no means patient with either my sister or myself, and would deplore our stupidity and tell us that we were 'enough to try the patience of Job!'

I remained unprogressively under her musical care for some two years, during which time I had the first great pianistic experience of my life; she had persuaded my mother to let her take me over to Liverpool to hear Paderewski.

I remember that Saturday afternoon vividly. The (old) Liverpool Philharmonic Hall – since burnt down – was filled to capacity. It was also filled, I noticed, with a murky haze, which was not altogether pleasing to my nostrils but which was soon forgotten when Paderewski began to play. He was thirty-one at the time and, with his great mop of auburn hair, was at the height of his popularity. I cannot give an account of that recital for obvious reasons, I can only say that it clinched my resolve to become a musician – and a long-haired one at that! Many years later when I was driving in a cab with Paderewski to his hotel, I told him of this resolve (without any reference, of course, to hair) whereupon he leant forward and pressed my hand. 'May it bring you luck', he said.

Strange to say it was through this recital that I indirectly made a discovery. Great artist though he was, Paderewski had a deplorable habit of preluding all his items with the dominant seventh chord of the key in which he was about to play. In the days when I first heard him in Liverpool, his *Minuet in G* had become a popular piece and he would often give it as an encore, in fact he did so at that very recital. On our way home I said to Miss B, 'I knew he was going to play his Minuet.' 'How could you know?' she asked. 'Because of those chords he played in

B

the key of G beforehand.' 'Good Gracious!' she exclaimed,
'that means you've got absolute pitch!' – which was quite
true, though its possession is a mixed blessing. Whether, after
this discover, Miss B. came to entertain more respect for me as a
budding musician, she did not reveal; and soon after, I lost
touch with her. But I did hear through my sister that she
subsequently married a man who turned out to be quite ineffective as a bread-winner, and so she was obliged to go on
giving lessons to the end of her days.

When I had reached the age of ten, my parents decided to
send me to a day-school. Thus, my mother one day announced
that I was to go to 'Mrs. Dagnall's', and took pains to point
out what a good school it was and how much I should enjoy
being with other children; in short, she stuffed me with the
usual nonsense in case I should give voice to any protests. And
this I would certainly have done if I had guessed what was in
store for me. For I came to hate not only the lessons but the
playground as well, in which I was bullied by boys stronger
than myself who threatened to 'lick' me if I did not accede to
their demands to yield up sundry of the postage stamps I
collected and other of my possessions. As for the teacher, Miss
Dagnall, she was a powerful disciplinarian, but had no idea of
making the lessons in the least interesting. Altogether I consider my schooldays one of the most unpleasant experiences in
my life, and when people talk of the happiness of their own
schooldays I can only think they were unusually lucky or are
just talking nonsense.

CHAPTER VI

Regarding Matters of Sentiment and Sex

LIKE many musicians who have Venus in a prominent place in their horoscopes, I started my 'love affairs' early – I could only have been about four or five when Cupid began to aim his arrows at me. My first tender sentiments were awakened by a tall, long-nosed girl of eighteen, of whom I can recall very little except that she indirectly acted as a soporific, in that after being put to bed at night I would conjure up her image until I pleasantly glided into sleep.

The first *amour* lasted a few months and then died a natural death, after which I oscillated between states of being in and out of love more or less till my first reciprocated romance in my sixteenth year with a girl of my own age. I say reciprocated, yet it was only in spirit, for the whole romance was conducted with such propriety that not a single kiss was exchanged. Although the dictionary defines calf love – of which this was an obvious example – as a silly boyish or girlish love, I am far from certain that it isn't the definition which is silly, seeing that at one time I was under the delusion that calf love had something especially to do with legs! Moreover, whether such loves are silly or not, they can nonetheless be very intense and painful while they last. Indeed, my eventual parting from this girl was so poignant that I shed many bitter tears.

Why I should have fallen so painfully in love with a flapper who was not at all pretty is one of those commonplace mysteries pertaining to all romantic love, for which orientals would say the doctrine of reincarnation alone offers a satisfying explanation – in one sentence, we tend to love again those we have loved before in a previous rebirth, and have re-met.

But however that may be, where amativeness as such is con-

cerned, I cannot agree with Bernard Shaw that nothing whatever can be learnt about a man from his love affairs. Nevertheless, this much may perhaps be conceded, namely that a
person's sexual or sentimental idiosyncrasies may often be no
indication of his or her real character. One of my own while still
in my teens was the naïve wish to see a pretty girl weep, and to
fancy myself as her comforter! I have never happened to come
across persons who confessed to a similar paradoxical peculi-
arity, but I have known several people of blameless character
who owned to having sexual 'kinks' of which, according to
sexologists, there are an enormous variety. These most often
originate at a very early age, and though many of them may be
quite harmless, even so may become, if very peculiar, a considerable nuisance in manhood.

For this reason, during the first world war when matters of
sex were still regarded with hypocritical intolerance, I was unwise enough to write an anonymous book in the hopes of
creating that understanding which in accordance with the
French proverb is said to be the prerequisite to pardoning. But,
alas, for my good intentions. Oscar Wilde's friend the late Lord
Alfred Douglas of all people, brought an action against its
publishers, who were ordered to burn the whole edition. One
aspersion cast on me in Court – and not being present I could
not refute it – was that had my intentions been really altruistic I
would have written the book under my own name. Queer
reasoning, considering that most of the intimate revelations had
been confided to me by several of my friends, who in that case
might have been identified! . . . I was sorry for the publishers,
but it was largely their own fault for badgering me to add details
and notes which were not in the original script. I warned them
that we might be 'sailing too near the wind', but I was over-
ruled. The book was certainly no masterpiece, and when
correcting the proofs I was careless enough to overlook such a
comical atrocity as 'he smelt a rat which soon became a
certainty'!

Mention of Oscar Wilde reminds me that anything in the

nature of homosexuality has always been entirely foreign to my temperament. Indeed, I owe it to Occultism for eventually ridding me of a strong intolerance towards homosexuals and lesbians by explaining its basic occult cause. Not that I ask the reader to accept it; but as this book is concerned with confessions of beliefs as well as others, I give it nonetheless. Briefly worded; when an entity has had several incarnations in succession as a woman, and when for certain reasons is obliged to incarnate as a man, then, being unable to adapt itself properly to the male body, the result is what is facetiously called 'a pansy', who is really a misfit, just as in the case of the opposite sex the lesbian is likewise a misfit. True, not all homosexuals are 'pansies'; yet when homosexual practices have been in past lives resorted to by men, monks for instance, isolated from women, the abnormality is apt to reappear in later ones.

To sum up this digression on matters of sex, I confess to the opinion that whilst of course sex has it natural importance, it has in addition acquired the *wrong sort* of importance; hence the countless tragedies, divorces, suicides and murders.

CHAPTER VII

Some of my Relations

ONE is unfortunate in one's relatives if they do not include a few characters, and such could my Uncle Tom and my Aunt Louise be called. Both of them were associated with my first visit to London at quite an early age. They lived in one of those huge, high houses overlooking Clapham Common, which had been built in the hopes that Members of Parliament would elect to live there; hopes, however, that were not fulfilled.

My aunt was a voluminous lady with auburn hair, double chin, retroussé nose, a haughty, throaty voice and the manners of a stage duchess. Her method of making pleasant conversation was to pay people scores of compliments. How she could think of them all was a miracle, and how many of the payees were taken in by them would depend on their respective degree of vanity. She was a completely worldly woman, and when years later I asked her what would be her idea of heaven, she said "Rotten Row in Hyde Park", and to relive the happy days she had spent there when young and courted by many swains! Although she pretended to hate the London Season with its endless succession of 'At Homes' and parties, I noticed that she and my uncle were among the first to arrive at such functions and among the last to leave; at any rate at those to which they took me when I had reached a suitable age, and before I settled down in London on my own.

Why my Aunt Louise had chosen to marry so pious a man as my Uncle Tom may have been a mystery to some of her associates, for both in build and outlook he was entirely her opposite, being a tall, spare man with a bald head, across which a few wisps of hair were extended and plastered down with some pomade. He had a large nose and a short, pointed beard, dyed with some substance which unfortunately tinged it with a greenish hue and so dispelled any illusion that he had obviously wished to create. On one occasion I even remember him dyeing his hair and beard a brilliant golden colour, much to the annoyance of his widowed daughter, who in consequence refused to go out with him. He was then nearly eighty, my aunt having died a few years previously . . .

One might wonder how he reconciled all this preoccupation with his personal appearance with his religious beliefs and activities, for nothing gave him greater pleasure than church services, prayer-meetings, missionary meetings and any sort of strictly protestant gatherings. But then, as my aunt said to me; 'With your uncle, religion is a dissipation'. Certainly, to do him full justice, he was no 'gloomoid', and if he took his religious pleasures seriously, it cannot be said that he took them sadly. Indeed, he was something of a comedian, having a type of wit peculiar to himself. Yet his sense of humour deserted him where religion was concerned and gave place to an astonishing naïvety; for in addition to the numerous framed texts hanging on the walls of every bedroom, he had hung one large one in the W.C. of all places, bearing the three ill-chosen words, 'God sees you'!

Although I remember this eccentric uncle with affection, it was fortunate for me that at the period of my life when I saw him most frequently I had already acquired some very decided ideas about art, otherwise he might have proved a distinctly bad influence. He tried to persuade me that the value of a musical composition could only be gauged by the amount of money it brought in! – a contention I found so sordid and untrue that I did not even bother to refute it. Of course, if a piece of music does bring in some money – well – that is very gratifying, but I have never been interested in money-making *per se*, and certainly have never tried to increase the meagre weight of my purse through my compositional activities. True, for a number of years, I had to fulfil certain obligations to my publisher and this meant writing a few potboilers; but of these and their outcome I will deal later, for in some respects they proved my undoing.

Meanwhile, to finish off in a literary sense my 'duchessy' Aunt Louise, looking back at the times spent in her company, I realise that she contributed quite a useful item to my education in that she taught me much about the vagaries and vanities of human nature as it was in the 'naughty nineties' and as to a large extent it has remained. Granted that today we are not the hypocrites that many of my Victorian compatriots were, yet as conventions have altered there is no need for such hypocrisy. Not that my aunt was a hypocrite herself, hence did she the better teach me to see through other people's hypocrisies: the more subtle sort not always associated with religion. Her own religious outlook was quite a reasonable one. Although she accompanied my uncle by way of humouring him to some of the prayer-meetings and similar functions, she told me that whilst she did believe in a good and loving God, she could not believe that He demanded such naïve attentions. She died a few years before my uncle, and on the way back from her burial he made the curious remark: 'I don't like to think of poor Louise all alone in that grave'.

I fear that for the entertainment of the reader I cannot unearth any interesting relatives in the form of criminals, drunkards, libertines and the like, but I can at least give a brief and inadequate pen-sketch of my Uncle George. As a youngish man he had had a terrible mishap. While practising archery – a most harmless form of sport – he had fallen backwards and so injured his spine that for over forty years he was doomed to lie on a wheeled couch until he died. Moreover he could not even be wheeled about in the street but only from the house to a little plot of garden, because any jolting caused him intense suffering. During these years he sustained the loss of his wife and the youngest of his three sons (who was killed in the first world war) and yet nobody ever heard him rail against this fate, which he accepted with such patience that 'the Canon' was wont to say: 'To visit Mr. George Scott is a sermon in itself'!

Incidentally, for the interest of Liverpudlians, one of his three sons, Gilbert Scott – not the architect of that name – was the only contractor who could be found to undertake the dangerous job of pulling down the New Brighton (Eiffel) Tower.

CHAPTER VIII

First Visit to Germany

ALTHOUGH my father took a gloomy view of music as a career for me, far from standing in the way of my ambition, he allowed me to go to Germany – then regarded as the most musical country in the world – when I was only twelve years of age. Moreover, he hoped that a prolonged stay in 'The Fatherland' would be to the good of my general education. Frankfurt am Main was the town selected, and as my sister was not to be left out of this wise educational scheme, she was to be placed in a school in a near-lying Spa.

As my father could not leave his business, and the matter of finding a suitable family for me to live with might take some time, it was decided that my mother should make the journey with us. She did not know a word of German, but fortunately she was slightly acquainted with a German spinster who happened to be travelling back to her home at that time and was going via Frankfurt.

Thus, one winter's morning in 1891 I was faced with a particularly poignant leave-taking; and even my stoic father had tears in his eyes when he saw us off at the station. Trying to cheer us up, I remember him saying: 'A man was hanged this morning for murder. That after all is much worse than this.'

Of the journey I can only recall a few details; that we had a bad and bilious crossing; that at Flushing I observed a quaint notice with the words *Take care for pickpockets*; that having finally arrived at Frankfurt and put up for the night at the biggest hotel, I was astonished at the amazing thickness and weight of the breakfast cups!

The first day was spent in walking the streets in search of a *pension*, the good German spinster-lady trudging along through the snow with us to act as interpreter. Catching sight of a doorplate marked *Pension Steiner*, my mother wondered if the guest-house it indicated would suit our purposes? 'It might, if you have no objection to boarding with Jews', said our *cicerone;* and as my parent had none, the matter was soon settled . . . 'Having let ourselves down', as the Germans say, I received my first lessons in the German language from a not unprepossessing young Jewess with raven hair and swarthy complexion, who was one of the inmates. At meals we all sat at a long table, during which some of our fellow guests took the opportunity of airing their English – such as it was – by way of putting my mother a little at her ease. They also made all sorts of helpful suggestions; Frau Scott should take her small son to the Opera; she should take him to hear *Lohengrin* which was to be given a few days hence and was Wagner's greatest Opera(?); she should also take him to the beautiful *Palmengarten*, and so on and so-forth. And my mother, who had never heard an opera in her life, did take me to hear *Lohengrin* – though I think all the time she may have had the uncomfortable feeling that Canon Robson might not altogether have approved.

Those were the days when Julius Stockhausen (friend of Brahms and Joachim, if I remember rightly) was regarded as *the* great singing teacher, and to whom would-be professional vocalists came from almost all parts of the globe. He was then at the apex of his career and did much of his teaching in Frankfurt, where he eventually died. Staying at the *pension*, together with her widowed mother, was one of his American pupils, a young woman with a remarkable voice but with such an unengaging appearance that I very much doubt whether she ever made a career. This couple became our almost constant companions, and as they knew a little German, we found them exceedingly useful when it came to the momentous business of getting me enrolled as a pupil at the Conservatorium.

The Principal at that time was *Herr Direktor* Dr. Bernard

Scholz, an imposing and awe-inspiring old gentleman with a very florid face and longish white hair, who walked with a slow, shuffling gait and usually wore a black frock coat quite incongruous with the rest of his attire, which was of a bile-coloured texture without any pattern. Before this frightening apparition I had one morning to display my talents on the platform of the empty concert-hall of the Conservatoire building. I don't know who was the most nervous, my mother or myself, but despite my dithers I evidently contrived to impress the old man, for after having put me through some ear-tests, he fetched one of the professors, for whom I had to go through my paces once again. The upshot was – so my mother was informed – that whilst as a general rule no pupil was admitted to the Conservatoire at so young an age, in view of 'the young Herr's' unusual talent, an exception would be made in this case, and lessons could start almost at once. My piano professor was to be Herr Uzielli, and for so-termed *theory* (a silly term) I was to be placed in the class of Herr Humperdinck.

At that time the Hochs'che Conversatorium was one of the best in the country and numbered several artists of considerable reputation among its teachers. There was the cellist Hugo Becker for one, and the violinist Hugo Heermann for another. Becker possessed very decided ideas on cello-playing, and when eventually Casals appeared in the musical arena, the mere mention of him was sufficient to upset his emotional equilibrium to a considerable degree. As for Hugo Heermann, whom I came to know well in later years when he was an old man, his temper was as sweet as the tone he coaxed out of his violin and for which he was noted. But as he ventured to kiss some of his lady pupils as well as instruct them, his appointment at the Conservatoire came to a somewhat untimely end. In vain did his wife – a delightful, breezy, warm-hearted Argentinian – expostulate with the *Herr Direktor*, telling him it was absurd to make a fuss about a mere kiss; he remained adamant and would tolerate no improprieties. Moreover, other complaints had been made: yet considering that there were always two students present at every lesson, whether the complaints were lodged by the pupil who had been kissed or out of pique by the one who had not received these attentions, I never discovered.

Nor was it always the morals of the teachers who gave the old Direktor disturbed nights; I remember one ex-*prima donna* who had to be got rid of because of the violence of her temper and the uncouthness of her language when displeased with her pupils. Thus in view of all that the good *Herr Direktor* had to contend with, perhaps it was not so strange that to toughen himself, and by way of a change of unpleasantnesses, every Sunday, wet or fine, he would toil up to the top of the highest mountain of the *Taunus Gebirge* with such cronies as he could induce to go with him. Or perhaps through these exertions he hoped to acquire inspiration for his compositions, which, as they stood, were too tediously correct to be attractive. In any case he was an imposing figure and an admirable Principal, and although, because of his pedantry, I may have reasons to be thankful that I was not one of his actual students, I nonetheless owe him a debt of gratitude for the way he handled my case at the outset.

CHAPTER IX

A Strange Family

THE next step was to find the right sort of family to board me, and so my mother approached the British chaplain, who turned out to be an aged Scotsman, addicted, as I was soon to learn, to preaching, so to say, hell-fire sermons of a most depressing nature. The family he recommended with confidence I will call by the name of Seiler. It consisted of Herr, Frau and Fräulein S., who lived in a flat of no large dimensions, yet who nonetheless managed to take in young Englishmen who wanted to learn the language. As a family they possessed, so I eventually discovered, the most peculiar characteristics, if that is not too mild a word.

'Old Seiler,' as my fellow P.Gs. irreverently called him, was a kindly, timid, weak-willed, sentimental old man with a short white beard, a rather large, broken nose, and a continually watering eye; the latter having resulted from a surgical attempt to rid him of neuralgia by extirpating one of his facial nerves. His wife was a plump, benign-faced woman with black hair, smoothed down and parted in the middle, over which she wore a small lace cap. Strangely enough she hailed from Liverpool, where she had been cashier in a café, from which conspicuous post Herr S. had rescued her in a matrimonial manner and taken her off to Germany some thirty years earlier. One of her minor peculiarities was that not only did she drop her aitches in English but also in German, which she had learnt to speak with considerable fluency. I remember on one occasion I happened to describe the appearance of some man I had met in the street, whereupon she asked; '*Wie 'eisst denn der 'Err?*' – the comicality of which only a German will appreciate.

On first acquaintance, judging from her exterior, one would

44

have taken her to be the most motherly, sweet-natured old lady it was one's good fortune to meet with when seeking a suitable guardian for a sensitive young lad. But beneath this pleasant surface-picture lurked another of a very different kind; that of a selfish, hard, self-dramatising woman, superstitiously religious yet possessing few of the real Christian attributes. Perhaps, for all I know, she tried to acquire them, but without any noticeable success. Be that as it may, the fact that her husband acted as churchwarden-cum-sidesman to the aged chaplain, and that she, together with her spouse and daughter, was a strict observer of the Sabbath, carried much weight with my mother who especially desired that I should not fall into 'those bad Continental Sabbath-breaking ways!'

As regards Frl. Seiler (with whom I was to form a friendship which lasted till her death at over eighty) she was a comely big-bosomed, red-haired young woman of twenty-six, with an alarmingly quick temper but with the warmest and kindest of hearts. Many years later when I used to stay with her and her husband, I was to make the discovery that she was of a very jealous temperament; a particularly unfortunate failing in view of the type of husband she was destined to acquire.

I had not been with the family Seiler for more than a few weeks when I began to notice some very peculiar things. But first I must explain that all the rooms of the flat opened on to a square *Vorplatz* (small hall), in one corner of which was the kitchen and in the opposite one the bedroom of Herr and Frau Seiler. Frau S. never appeared till one o'clock dinner time, and after that meal would recline on the sofa – there being a sofa in the dining room – till tea, then usually again till supper, after which we would on most evenings all sit round the table and play for my benefit 'Tiddleywinks'.

One morning when crossing the *Vorplatz* after breakfast, I made, through the carelessness of Herr S., a somewhat unappetizing discovery. He had left the bedroom door ajar, and through it I caught a glimpse of the old lady reclining in bed and engaged in preparing the salad for dinner. Indeed, it subse-

quently transpired that all such items for the midday meal that
could be prepared outside the kitchen were prepared by Frau
Seiler *in bed* . . . But I was soon to make yet another discovery;
it was that not only did Frau Seiler expect her husband to wait
on her hand and foot, but also to perform certain unpleasant
duties which generally speaking only professional nurses perform for very sick persons or bedridden invalids. In short, the
old woman was so self-indulgent and lazy, that for no purpose
whatever could she be induced to leave her bed till the day was
'well aired'.

Even so, the unsavoury habits of the Seiler parents would
have been something to giggle over if only I had had a companion to giggle with; but I had none, and so was lonely. The
warm-hearted Frl. Seiler was kind to me, yet was constantly
annoying me by sending me on errands, all doubtless very good
as discipline, but I resented being treated as a messenger-boy.
My annoyance reached a climax when one day she sent me
round with a bunch of flowers to a lady who, after I had rung
the bell, popped her head out of an upper window and, mis-
taking my errand, angrily bid me depart.

I had hoped that this indignity to my neatly dressed self
would teach Frl. S. a lesson. But not at all; she was merely
amused, and continued her practice of bouncing into my room
with her usual request: 'Ach, Cyrilsche, be so good as to run
round to Herr Schluckerbier and ask for . . .' etc. etc. In fact I
soon became known in all the small shops in the vicinity as 'the
little Englishman'. This being kindly meant did not trouble me
much. But what I disliked intensely was the reaction produced
in passers-by when on Sundays I had to go in my Eton suit; a
garb which my mother had insisted I should always wear going
to church. As nobody in Frankfurt had ever seen such a suit
except on waiters, I became the object of derisive amusement
on the part of all other small boys as I shamefacedly walked
along.

Despite the salad etc. having been dressed on Frau Seiler's
bed, the food in the Seiler family was much more appetizing

1. Myself in middle age. Taken during a concert tour in Canada.

2. My mother, Mary Scott (*née* Griffiths), soon after her wedding.

3. My father, Henry Scott. A biblical Greek scholar at 48.

4. Stefan George, the German poet. A friend during my teenage years, who greatly influenced my artistic life. Later I translated 200 of his poems into English.

than any I had so far tasted in England. And yet meals were not altogether a pleasant function because of Frau Seiler's silly play-acting – which, however, I was too young to assess as such. Although she was a thoroughly food-loving old woman, as a ruse to extract coaxings and cajoleries from her weak-willed husband she would pretend that she had a 'discordered stomach' and could eat nothing at all. And so, what with her whinings and complainings and her old man's distressed solicitude, while my tongue was tasting good food, my spirit was usually somewhat ill at ease. Being curious, like most small boys, I tried to discover from Frl. S. the nature of her mother's indisposition, but all I got (at that time) by way of answer was that 'little boys wouldn't understand'. Then one day while out for a walk with Herr Seiler's aged brother, who lived near by, the truth was revealed. 'Why,' I had asked, 'does Frau Seiler spend most of the day on the sofa? What is really the matter with her?' To which he quaintly replied in English: 'She complains of her womb.'

Until I came to live with this strange family I had never seen elderly people carry on in the demonstrative manner in which the Seiler parents behaved. Most evenings before supper they were to be seen reclining together on the sofa, Frau. S. at the upper and Herr S. at the lower end, his legs on a chair and his head pillowed on one of her fat thighs. Moreover, they were constantly holding hands and calling each other the most endearing names; the while they would extol themselves for my benefit as a perfect example of conjugal affection. Nevertheless the example seems to have been somewhat lopsided, for although the old lady could seldom refer without emotion to her own eventual passing, when a few years later her doting spouse died of pneumonia, not a single tear did she shed. "In fact," her daughter added when giving me this information, "I believe she was really glad, because she would have more money for herself."

Nevertheless, I should be doing an injustice to the three souls, who are doubtless enjoying the felicities of the Afterlife, if

I gave the impression that they had been unkind to me in any way. To the contrary, they had treated me well and even regarded me with affection, insipid and melancholy little boy that I was. Thus, although my mother could not possibly have divined all their peculiarities when arranging to leave me with them, she did at least judge rightly that I should be in safe and kind hands, and so could return to England without any misgivings. I can still remember her departure. She had come over to the Seiler's flat from her *pension*, I having already been installed there some days, and after chatting a bit and admonishing them to see that I washed my ears properly, she got up and, out of consideration for my feelings, merely remarked in a melodiously casual manner: 'Well – good afternoon, Cyril' . . . It was to be eighteen months before I saw her again.

CHAPTER X

My Three Teachers

I WAS told to my chagrin that my piano lessons with Herr
Uzielli were to take place at 8 o'clock in the morning, which
might not have been so bad in the summer, but in the winter
meant arriving at one's lesson, after a twenty-minutes walk,
with icy cold fingers incapable of performing their proper
function. As Herr Uzielli could not speak a word of English,
it was arranged that my fellow pupil should be an Englishman
named Holland-Smith who, knowing German quite well,
could act as interpreter. He was some fourteen years my senior
and was destined to become a life-long friend.

I now had to suffer the consequences of all the previous bad
and dishonest tuition. So as to undo all my bad habits, I was
put on five-finger exercises and not permitted to touch the
piano except for the purpose of practising them. No more
improvising, no more self-expressing – and this was to be for
some three months or more according to how I progressed.
The prospect was desolating!

Herr Uzielli was a Neapolitan by birth who had become a
naturalized German. He had been a pupil of Madame
Schumann, and taught the Schumann method of piano-playing.
Out of lessons he was a most lovable man, with deep brown,
kindly eyes, charming, open smile and expansive nature
characteristic of the warm-hearted Italian temperament; but
in the lessons somehow these attractive qualities seemed to
disappear. He had certain habits which made most of his pupils
feel so nervous that they failed to do justice to themselves, for
he would wiggle his foot and breathe in an audible, strained
manner, as if their performances were so intensely painful to
him that only with the greatest effort could he restrain himself

from exploding! To do him justice, he never flew into a temper, yet sometimes his scoldings could be acrimonious enough to provoke tears from many of his female pupils.

Apropos this, years later when I was staying with him and his second wife, and when he no longer held Conservatoire appointments and only gave private lessons, I had it out with him in a friendly manner. One day as he sat down to lunch, he had said, making a wry face, 'There were tears during the lesson this morning.' 'But why so severe?' I asked. 'It's not your fault if your pupil doesn't practise enough.' 'No', he said. 'But if I take her money, I have to do my duty as a teacher.' I did not pursue the matter, but thought and still think the principle is wrong. We pay our teachers to *teach* us and draw out the best in us, not to reduce us to a state of jitters so that we can neither play, sing or whatever it may be. For my own part I have had few pupils, but have always adopted the attitude: 'I'll do my best for you. But my best will be quite useless unless you co-operate with me. I shall not tear my hair if you don't work well. But in that case you won't get on; and that's all there is to it'. And because I adopted that attitude I think my pupils enjoyed their lessons; which is more than I did with Herr Uzielli – though I came to love him dearly when he was no longer my teacher. This is not to say that I feel no gratitude for what he taught me, but merely that his mode of imparting it might have been more effective and agreeable.

A very different personality was Humperdinck, in whose class I was placed for *theory*. He was a painfully ugly man with what the Germans uncharitably call a *Stink-nase*, i.e. a nose without any bridge to it. Of how to teach he had no conception at all, and was so absent-minded that he would go off into long brown studies, the while he would seem to be counting his fingers until recalled to his surroundings by a giggle or a cough from one of the students. Although he had acted as assistant to Wagner for a short period at Bayreuth, he had such a modest opinion of his own talents as a composer that his whole idea in writing *Hänsel und Gretel* was merely to amuse his children. Indeed, had not some of the professors at the Conservatoire – to whom he played portions of it – seen its possibilities and likelihood of becoming a popular opera, that charming work would in all probability never have reached the public at all, and Humperdinck would have remained the indigent, feckless man he was when he taught me how to make notes less suggestive of potatoes.

I have still to mention another of my teachers at that time; his name was Dr. Conrad Schmidt, and he was responsible for my more general education. I shared him, so to say, with a young mollycoddle of a boy named Karl O—, to whose domicile I had to go every morning for a few hours, much to my discomfort, seeing that I never knew what might be in store for me. I say this because I had not overcome the nervous agitation I always experienced when anybody was scolded, and as Karl O— was far from being mentally well equipped at that time, he came in for ratings on most days. I can still remember some of his howlers. He was taught both French and English, and sometimes he got them most comically mixed. Having been asked what was the English for *die Butterfrau*, he answered, 'the femme of butter!'

Herr Dr. Schmidt was a military type of man about sixty, with a waxed and nearly white moustache and silver grey hair. He held himself so straight that his back concaved in the lumbar region causing his buttocks to appear unduly prominent, whilst a tendency to be somewhat bow-legged detracted from his otherwise soldierly dignity. To make the lessons more pleasant for himself – though less so for us – he smoked cheap German cigars the whole time he instructed us, so that after a while our eyes began to smart and our clothes to reek of stale tobacco. Nevertheless he was a good, painstaking and kind-hearted man; who, when the time came after a year's tuition to bid me farewell, had tears in his eyes as he told me that to lose a pupil was like having a piece of flesh cut off his own body! – a somewhat more surgical than poetic simile, yet those were his exact words. But then he was a sad, lonely old man. There had been a tragedy in his life which had left its mark; he had fought through the Franco-Prussian war, had come home wounded from the terrible battle of the Sedan, only to find that the girl he was engaged to had just died.

Many times during the course of my life I have guiltily thought of this pathetic, harmless preceptor, for I am ashamed to say that associated with him is one of the most heartless and discreditable incidents of my career: when after an absence of some two years I returned to Frankfurt to complete my musical education, not only did I fail to visit the old man, but when one evening we came face to face in a café where I happened to be sitting, I cut him dead. And the less can I forgive myself for what was in part shyness, part gaucherie, because he was looking more sad, poor and lonely than ever, and the meeting with an old pupil might have cheered his melancholy soul. Though trite the saying, we humans are a mass of contradictions, otherwise how could I, who have been troubled with a painfully tender heart since childhood, have done something so completely heartless?

CHAPTER XI

I leave the Strange Family

M Y first visit to Germany lasted eighteen months, during
which time I did not return to England even in the long
summer holidays. During the first of the Easter vacations I was
invited to visit my sister at the girls' school where she was
enjoying a more or less happy existence. The good lady who
owned the school took me to her heart and occasionally pressed
me to her bosom, and being a small boy among a bevy of girls,
I was made more fuss of than was strictly good for me. There
was only one snag which marred my enjoyment; during the
nights I was tormented by an intolerable itching – I had been
put in a bed infested by bugs! A minor unpleasantness was a
disagreeable smell, that of chamber-pots which had been in-
sufficiently cleansed.

But at least I knew the cause of that particular smell, which
is more than I did when, sitting down one evening to supper
after a walk, I became aware of such an unsavoury odour that I
examined my boot-soles to see whether I had not stepped in
something. Finding them clean, I whispered to my sister that
she must have been careless. Whereupon it transpired that what
I was actually smelling was that pestiferous German aliment
called *Handkäse* (hand-cheese). Incidentally, one of the many
curious things about human beings is that, whereas many of
them are exceedingly particular how their foods *look* (they will
unwisely soda-ize vegetables to make them look green) they are
apparently quite indifferent as to how they smell.

To a young boy, a year and a half seems a long time, yet I
was not actually home-sick. But that is not to say that I did not
still suffer from fits of abysmal depression, during which it often
happened that I could not suppress my tears. Sometimes the

53

warm-hearted Frl. Seiler surprised me in this lachrymose condition, and regarding me with a puzzled compassion, would want
to know the cause of my grief. But as there was no palpable
cause and I did not know what to say, I finally invented one. I
told her that I was upset because I wished I were a better boy!
This outrageous piece of humbug and hypocrisy proved so
effective that one day I overhead her repeating it to one of her
friends. 'How sweet, how touching!' was the response; but for
my part I was intensely annoyed at having made myself appear
such a contemptible prig. I had learnt my lesson, thenceforth I
never resorted to that kind of stratagem again.

At that time the only individual who more or less understood
my freakish nature was my fellow pupil Holland-Smith. He
contrived to dispel my melancholy moods by taking me for
walks, excursions into the beautiful *Taunus Gebirge*, and even
sometimes to the Opera. As a character he was a most original
and enlivening person, with a very distinguished appearance
but some curious mannerisms, especially when playing the
piano. He had a habit of gyrating on the piano-stool and
indulging in other irrelevant antics which so became the despair
of Herr Uzielli that, unable to endure them any longer, he
would remind him in a pained voice: 'But Herr Smisz, one
does not play the piano with one's stomach' . . . . And yet
withal my friend possessed such a sense of humour that few
things amused him more than to see me mimic him, when he
would laugh till completely exhausted.

He lived in one of the first class *pensions*, and being English,
good-looking and unusual, he aroused the sentimental emotions
of his host's daughter who embarrassed him somewhat – though
I daresay he was secretly pleased – by leaving nosegays and
sentimental notes on his night-table. As he thought it unwise to
respond to these touching advances, the young lady became
jealous of my quite innocent self, imagining that I was in some
way the cause of his seeming frigidity.

It was Holland-Smith who first impressed on my young mind
the important fact that the prerequisite to becoming a com-

poser of any lasting merit is the capacity to evolve a style of one's own. This remark was apropos my compositional efforts at that period, which, by the way, had acquired a somewhat Bach-like tinge. I had even ventured to show one of them to Herr Uzielli, who in turn had shown it to the composition master, Iwan Knorr, and subsequently handed it back to me with the verdict: 'Quite nice, and showing talent'!

Unlike my own, Holland-Smith's musical ambitions were modest ones; he merely desired to take a post in a good school as master of music and modern languages. As he possessed all the qualifications for such a post, these ambitions were easily fulfilled, and he became for many years a much respected figure in a North of England boys' school. Hugh Walpole, by the way, was one of his scholars. Nevertheless, his end-of-term concerts were a little too successful to please the Reverend Head, who either was assailed with some twinges of unchristian envy, or, not caring for music himself, must needs regard it as an unfitting subject for so much enthusiasm. Not music, but cricket was what made boys manly; cricket was something to be taken seriously, but music – tut, tut!

Holland-Smith and I remained close friends until his death during the last war at over eighty. As a tribute to his memory I eventually presented a Burne-Jones window to a non-conformist chapel in Exford. Not that he was a non-conformist himself, nor that I (being a Universalist) can specifically be called one; but as I had reason to believe that the worship in that particular chapel was truly heart-felt and sincere, more-over the interior was dismally plain, I thought the gift a suitable one. Besides which, I had lived for a while at Exford in the early nineteen-forties, and possessed pleasant memories of the little village.

To revert to Frankfurt. The year and a half having nearly passed, my parents came over to take my sister and myself home again; for my general education had to be considered. Incidentally, Frl. Seiler was to be married to a romantic widower and carried off to the South of France.

I have heard it said that it is a bad policy for a man to marry his deceased wife's best friend, though why it should be, I am not in a position to say. In any case, Mr. Vohl (as I shall call him) was willing to take the risk, and accordingly married Mathilda Seiler who had stood in that relationship to the late Mrs. Vohl.

I was not destined to see the wedded couple again for many years – and in very different circumstances. But of that later.

CHAPTER XII

Home Again

W HEN I left Frankfurt I had no idea that I would eventually return there, nor had my father, nor Herr Uzielli who, thinking he was to lose his pupil for good, had mournfully remarked: 'One gives oneself the trouble, and then—'

Much as I had loved the woods and the beautiful surroundings of Frankfurt, one of the first things I realised when I arrived back in England was how greatly I had missed the smell of the sea. As *The Laurels* had been let furnished for a while and was not quite ready for our reception, my parents had taken rooms in New Brighton at the mouth of the Mersey. How good it was to walk along the shore with the scent of seaweed in one's nostrils and reflect that in front of one stretched several weeks of holidays!

But doubtless my parents' reflections were not quite so simple . . . or pleasant. They were faced with the complex problem of educating a freak of a son who was too sensitive to be sent to school, and at the same time of finding a first-class professor of the piano and one for harmony and counterpoint. The final upshot was that by dint of making inquiries at the Liverpool University College, as it then was, my father heard of an ex-headmaster who had fallen on evil days and in consequence was glad to act as tutor to lads in my sort of predicament. As for a piano-professor, an Austrian named Steudner-Welsing was recommended by one of my mother's friends, and in his musical care I was eventually placed.

Mr. Welsing was a little dumpling of a man with a large egg-shaped head like one of those obese Chinese idols to be seen in curio shops. He had a shortish sandy beard, and wore pince-nez which wobbled as he played. He spoke English fluently but in a curiously staccato manner which nonetheless had a certain comic charm. At heart he was an artist, but he had two deplorable habits; he jammed down the pedal and would often forget to release it, and further he snorted violently all the time he performed. Admittedly there are other pianists who snort; but that is all the more reason why every pupil with such a tendency should be taught at the outset to breathe properly, one of the essentials being to sit straight instead of bent double over the keyboard . . . I am here reminded of a female vocalist who came to sing in Frankfurt, but who brought with her an accompanist whose antics and contortions were so grotesque, that the listeners wellnigh forgot all about the vocal part of the performance, so intent were they on watching the 'monkey' at the piano. As a cynic remarked afterwards: 'There can only be one reason why a singer can tolerate such an accompanist – she must be in love with him!'

But to return to Mr. Welsing. One was not always quite sure of getting one's lesson, for the poor little man suffered from an inordinate craving for spirits, and to the despair of his landlady would sometimes vanish into space for days on end, leaving no indication of his whereabouts. Fortunately for me he taught me none of his bad habits but only some useful ones. By dint of making me play duets with him, he taught me to read fairly rapidly at sight. All the same, I hated those duet performances, for whenever I made mistakes, which was most of the time, he would violently lose his temper and so cause me to make them all the more. I remained his pupil for about two years. Eventually he left Liverpool and returned to Vienna, where I saw him for the last time in 1913. He had wisely taken unto himself a strong-minded wife who had weaned him from his deleterious habits.

My tutor, Mr. Jeaffreson, was the first preceptor I had who contrived to make me feel at ease, and for that very reason I endeavoured, out of gratitude, to please him. And so, I think, did the boy who shared the lessons with me. Mr. J. kept us in order for the simple reason that we had no desire *not* to be kept

in order. He made jokes, put on no school-masterly side, criticized Shakespeare, smoked his pipe and allowed himself to be
entirely natural. In his former capacity as schoolmaster this
sort of thing had not gone down at all, and he had been a dismal
failure. Of tragic sorrow in his life he had had a double share,
for he had lost both his sons; one, a soldier had been killed
abroad, and the other, a sailor, had been shipwrecked and
drowned. His wife was alive; a kindly soul, but like many
members of her sex, without conscience when a craving to talk
assailed her. For then, uninvited, she would come into the room
and interrupt the lessons with her babble about nothing, until
her husband, aching to get rid of her would say: 'The interview
is now ended'. Incidentally, I have often wondered how much
business would be done if men had their offices at home!

As Mr. Jeaffreson lived some distance from the Liverpool
landing-stage, once a month my father would give me a sum of
money for bus fares. Every morning, Saturdays and Sundays
excepted, he and I would walk the two-and-a-half miles down
to the Birkenhead Ferry, cross over by the boat, and then I
would make my way to Mr. J's abode. However, realising that
if I used my legs the bus-fare money could be spent in a more
pleasurable manner, I would trudge all the uphill way on foot.
I of course refrained from mentioning this profitable arrangement to my father, but might well have done so, for when he
found me out, instead of rating me soundly, he was delighted.
Had he not repeatedly impressed on me that exercise, exercise
and yet again exercise was the great secret of health?!

Being an occultist who cannot accept the theory of Chance as
a rational explanation for many happenings (why, I shall explain later), I believe that it was no mere coincidence, though
on the surface it appeared as such, that on most mornings while
a young lad was to be seen toiling up Bold Street on his way to
his tutor, a certain middle-aged Swiss gentleman named Hans
Lüthy would be walking in the opposite direction down to his
business. I (the young lad) did not notice *him*, but he noticed
me, and was soon to play an important part in my emancipa-

tion. . . . We eventually became acquainted at a musical soirée to which Mr. Welsing had contrived to get me invited; and as Mr. Lüthy was a man of action, he presented himself at my father's office the very next morning. The encounter was evidently harmonious, for my parent – who maybe was flattered – raised no objection to my accepting invitations to the Lüthy household. Mr. L. had explained that he and his wife had 'taken a fancy to me', that they were both enthusiastic music-lovers, that I should always receive a warm welcome at their home, and so on and so forth.

Thereafter began a friendship which was to last some twelve years; though I am certain that neither of my parents would have countenanced it had they guessed that the cultured and agreeable cornbroker was shortly to undermine all my religious orthodoxy and transform me into one of those 'godless and sadly misguided unbelievers'! And yet, strange to say, although Mr. L. was a pronounced agnostic, nothing moved him more than religious music of the higher type, especially that of Bach.

He had in his house, in addition to a grand piano, one of those better-class American organs on which for his entertainment I would treat him to choral-sounding and mock fugal improvisations. On the piano, when my small stock of Bach pieces was exhausted, I would improvise à la Bach or Handel and humbug him into believing that he was listening to the genuine article. After all, I argued, what does it matter if I do hoax him a bit, nobody is harmed by it? The only thing that in consequence I was not quite easy about was the fact that he credited me with possessing a huge repertoire and a pheno-menal memory!

Yet if Hans Lüthy had some illusions about myself at that time, he was a man with few illusions about human nature in general – of which he held a very poor opinion, one of his dicta being that most ways of making money were more or less dishonest. As for his own business, he said he was paid to do the dirty work of 'respectable' firms who were ashamed to do it for themselves; namely to engage in a form of gambling which in

his opinion was much worse than the straightforward Monte
Carlo type. Of church-goers he said: 'they pray to God on
Sundays and then try to get the better of their neighbours
during the rest of the week. Yes. And, my boy, remember this,'
he would say, 'most people are very vain. And if you ask a
favour of them, which you'll have to do many times if you want
to get on in the world, don't forget to softsoap their beards –
and lay it on thick.' These words of worldly wisdom, and many
more in the same vein, would be uttered during the many
outings on which he took me – sometimes as far as Wales for a
weekend.

In the earliest days of our association (when I had recently
been confirmed), he did not tamper with my religious convictions; that process was to come a little later. For one thing it
involved the reading of books, and had my parents caught me
studying such literature, some very awkward revelations would
have occurred. In any case, regarded from the ethical angle, it
is a moot point as to whether the Lüthys played fair with my
parents in luring me from the path they (especially my mother)
fervently desired that their son should tread. Yet to do Mr L.
and his wife justice, they thought it was wrong and hampering
to my mental development that I should accept without
questioning what *they* considered to be a tissue of lies.

Consequently, as soon as I was near to going abroad for the
second time, they began to plant seeds of doubt in my mind,
which was no very difficult matter in view of my youth. I was
then sixteen and quite unread, so during the next three years
Mr. Lüthy posted to Frankfurt such books as he deemed
essential for 'the good of my soul' – though, incidentally, he did
not believe that we humans have souls at all. Among those he
sent me were Ingersoll's *Mistakes of Moses*, popular books on
science, books on the so-termed higher criticism of the New
Testament and others of an agnostic nature. I had been taught
by Canon Robson that the Bible was the 'inspired Word of God',
and hence that every word of it must be true. But considering
that the Gospel narratives differed in many details, as I was

soon to discover, I began to think that Mr. Lüthy's disbeliefs were on a sounder footing than the worthy Canon's convictions. Moreover, much of the Bible was quite incompatible with the findings of science, which maintained (as I imagined) that the whole human population consisted of nothing more exalted than glorified monkeys, who after they had experienced their respective spans of life were snuffed out into nothingness.

All this seemed eminently satisfactory. If we were only super-apes, then there was no God to bother about, to placate, to pray to, to sing doggerel hymns to, and no after-life, either pleasant or unpleasant, to go to when we died; God and heaven and hell were simply inventions of the 'glorified monkeys', the result of superstition and fairy-tale spinning. As death meant complete unconsciousness, unconscious people could never be unhappy – in fact they had ceased to be people in every respect! ... Thus, accepting all this as undeniable Truth(!) I became that contradiction in terms, a dogmatic agnostic. It was not merely a question of 'we don't know', but 'we know that, apart from what science tells us, there is nothing *to* know'.

Of course, what I failed to realise was that the alluring doctrine of Agnosticism was largely based on inductive logic, which is plausible enough as long as no inconvenient facts come to light; but if they do, then they may upset the whole argument . . . at any rate for honest thinkers. (Dishonest ones try to explain them away).

Years later, when I had acquired some knowledge of Occultism, I learned that the Agnostic Movement had been purposely inspired by one of the Initiates of The Heirarchy in order to counteract the Victorian, illogical, false, gloomy and mischievous intrepretation of the Christian Religion of that epoch.*

And so, when all is said, Mr. Lüthy did me a service when he set about demolishing my beliefs. Agnosticism was a necessary step in my evolution, and for reasons to be mentioned later, I am glad that I went through that phrase of scepticism. I may

* I refer to this in my book *An Outline of Modern Occultism* (Routledge).

add that Mr. L. himself – who had repudiated any form of metaphysics all his life – finally ended, in his old age, as a Christian Scientist. But this was many years after our association had regrettably come to a discordant close. Some of my views had become too much even for *him* to swallow – besides, there were other considerations.

CHAPTER XIII

Back in Frankfurt

MR. Welsing and Mr. Jeaffreson had not been my only teachers, I had received harmony lessons from one of the local organists. But the unfortunate man developed a lingering and fatal illness and the lessons came to a sorrowful end. One day my mother received a letter from his wife telling her the bad news and suggesting that I should go for a last farewell lesson; but as I was so distressed at having to endure such a harrowing ordeal, my understanding mother had to explain matters as best she could.

I was then placed in the hands of another local organist who tried to teach me to avoid writing *consecutive fifths* and other musical improprieties, to which nowadays no composer pays the least attention. Meanwhile I had become far more interested in composing than in piano-playing, and for this reason I begged my father to let me return to Frankfurt in order to study with Iwan Knorr who was reputed to be one of the finest composition teachers then known. And so it ended in my going back to that beautiful city when I was verging on seventeen.

After teaching myself, from books, the rudiments of *form*, I had ambitiously composed a *Piano Trio* in the hopes of impressing Knorr at my first lesson. But, alas, for my conceit, my hopes were not to be fulfilled. 'As an indication of talent', he said, 'the effort is considerable. But as a work of art it is nothing.' So much for trying to learn composition from books!

I wrote some paragraphs anent this remarkable and original personality in *My Years of Indiscretion*,* from which in part I now quote:

*Mills & Boon. 1928.

64

Iwan Knorr was no cut-and-dried German music professor; he had lived many years in Russia, looked like a Russian, had married a Russian woman, and had been able to count Tchaikowski among his few friends. Although neither haggard nor anaemic-looking, he was of slender build, of sallow complexion, wore his iron grey hair *en brosse*, and had a short non-pointed and rather mangy-looking beard. His mode of dress was unaesthetically striking; he wore elastic-sided boots with imitation buttons, a cravat which looked as if two pieces of nondescript stuff had been glued on to a bit of cardboard (which I believe they *had*) a black jacket, browny-yellow trousers, and out of doors, a pork-pie hat without the customary indentation. In fine, he looked anything but smart. But he was unusually smart with his tongue, and his stuffy classroom was often the scene of embarrassments and blushes as the result of his witty sarcasms.

One of the secrets of Knorr's excellence as a teacher was that he never discouraged originality if it was in good taste. He told us that we must of course learn the rules – though not for the purpose of slavishly following them for the rest of our lives. But he did say, wittily and wisely, 'What you compose for me merely as exercises, do not write with your heart's-blood!'

Being now old enough to dispense with the protection of a family, old Herr Seiler found me a bed-sitting-room in the flat of a certain Fräulein Diehl, an elderly woman he had known for some time.

The only other inmate of the flat was a young man she introduced to me as her brother. But as he was about thirty years her junior, this fraternal relationship caused me some bewilderment. Not that it mattered, for I was quite comfortable; the place was clean and Frl. D. treated me kindly. As I dislike moving when once settled in a place, I had hoped that I might stay put for some time. But not so. For while I was away on my first summer holidays, Frl. D. took, as it were, the opportunity to die. I had even got so far, after arriving back, as to unpack my trunk, when a woman from the flat above entered the room and said: 'Have you not heard?' 'Heard what?' I asked. 'That Frl. Diehl is dead.' My face fell. What was to become of me now?

However, her 'brother' who (old Seiler subsequently confessed) was really her so-termed natural son, allowed me to stay on until I had found other accommodation – which I eventually did in the abode of two very dear but very aged maiden ladies. One of them, whenever she came into my little parlour, would nearly always make the same remark. Contemplating my *hired* grand piano, she would say: 'But Herr Schcott, what a magnificent instrument you have!'

Herr Uzielli had given me a heart-warming welcome. He invited me to lunch at his flat so that I might meet his wife and three very Italian-looking young sons.

Frau Julia Uzielli (a Genevese) was at the time a mezzo-soprano of some eminence, a strikingly beautiful woman and a fine artiste, with whom at a much later date I was to enjoy a very agreeable friendship (albeit of a strictly platonic nature). She then confided to me that Herr U. with his Neapolitan jealousy had been a very difficult husband to cope with, especially for a singer who had perforce to be frequently in the public eye. To complicate matters, she was one of those women who could not help blushing whenever any man looked at her admiringly. It even became a painful business for her to walk with her husband in the street, for no sooner did a man look at her than Uzielli would jealously exclaim: 'You *know* that gentleman!'

Yet, in the end, it was Uzielli himself who became the erring one for, when his wife's beauty began to fade, he became infatuated with a prepossessing young German woman, and subsequently married her. The scandal, however, necessitated his leaving Frankfurt and moving to Cologne, where he became one of the professors at the Conservatoire. Fortunately no bad blood had been created, and when after my student days were over I paid periodical visits to Germany, I would first stay with

Frau Uzielli No. 1 and her three sons, and then immediately proceed to Cologne to stay with my ex-teacher and Frau Uzielli No. 2. Nor did the first world-war disrupt our friendship. When my opera *The Alchemist* was (in 1928) given in Essen, the warm-hearted couple bothered to make the train journey in order to be present.

My student days in Frankfurt lasted some three years, at the end of which Knorr said to me: 'Well, you are going now. But it is perhaps for the best. I, for my part, feel that I should henceforth only be a hindrance to you instead of a help.' Words which showed the broadmindedness of the man. Although he knew that I should soon be coming back to Frankfurt, albeit not to study any more, there were tears in his eyes when he bade me farewell. And as for myself, I suffered acutely, also, when I came to take leave of Herr Uzielli.

I have recently heard from one of his sons that he died in 1943 from pneumonia at the age of eighty-two, his second wife having passed over earlier as the result of a long and painful illness. Their flat in Cologne had been bombed, but they were both away from home at the time. Towards the end he had wellnigh completely lost his memory, did not realise that his wife had departed and also that he had lost some intimate friends during the bombing of Cologne. His death, in Bonn, was peaceful.

CHAPTER XIV

'The Frankfurt Group'

IT was during the years in Frankfurt that I first made contact with that spate of composers since referred to as 'The Frankfurt Group'. Its members were Roger Quilter, Norman O'Neill, Percy Grainger and Balfour Gardiner – all of them very distinctive personalities. If Quilter had not been a musician he could have made a career as a comedian of a most original type, for he had a species of wit entirely his own. He was often in trouble with his staid, German landladies, but less because of his drolleries than because of other charming attributes. Like St. Francis of Assisi he had great compassion for the little birds, and every morning would put a lavish supply of crumbs for them out on his window-sill. But unfortunately, having eaten their fill, they would leave their 'visiting cards' on the slab, which so incensed his house-proud landlady, that one day she stormed into his room and told him she would stand it no longer. '*Most* unrefined!' she exclaimed.

The warm friendship with Quilter, which began in our student days, lasted until his death. Of Norman O'Neill I saw less in Frankfurt than I did when subsequently we had both settled in London.

O'Neill was one of the most good-looking men I have ever met, and certainly an extremely amusing one too. Although serious *au fond*, he appeared to take nearly everything in life as a joke, including myself. My philosophical outlook, my interest in Occultism, almost everything I said or did, he treated as subjects for intense amusement. With Irish blood in his veins he had an Irishman's wit. I remember him saying of a certain coarse-looking and obese music critic, since deceased, that he had 'a face like a bad smell'. So irrepressible was his sense of humour that when (in France) he married the pianist Adine Ruckert, he was overcome with merriment to such a degree during the ceremony that he was hard put to prevent his giggles from becoming noticeable.

His wife, who became well known in the musical world, was equally endowed with that blessed attribute, but with this difference, that with her I could discuss serious matters seriously, whereas with her husband, never. Doubtless she was often amused at some of my fads and fancies, yet at least she did not treat me as 'one huge joke', and even did me the honour of regarding me with affection. Moreover, she was a loyal friend of my music, as witness the following humorous incident. During the time she was head piano mistress at St. Paul's school for girls, a certain musician gave a talk on British composers for the keyboard. At the end of the lecture she rose up and said: 'But you have left out one of the most important – Cyril Scott.' Whereupon he answered: 'If I have done so, it is not because I don't recognise his talent, but because I consider his music of too licentious a character to be suitable for young girls!' It was she herself who, much to my amusement, told me about this incident.

Of Percy Grainger there is much to relate. Needless to say, thousands of people are now familiar with many of his works, yet I think only few of them know anything about the man himself. Apart from being extremely generous-handed, he is so generous-hearted and lavish with praise of his friends' works that I have at times been moved to point out that excessive praise may often defeat its own ends. To which, with his love of argument, he retorts that in America, where he lives, unless one 'piles it on thick' it makes no impression.

Nor is he less generous with his time and labour. During the 'thirties he spent hours altering the parts and score of my *Festival Overture* so as to make certain passages in it 'fool-proof'. He maintains: 'Nobody ever gets enough rehearsals for a new work, so score it so that it can't sound bad however badly it is rehearsed'! Incidentally, he himself has conducted the Overture in America and elsewhere, or been instrumental in getting it performed.

At the time of writing this chapter he is playing my *Piano Sonata No. 1* on tour – a work I wrote some forty-five years ago. With his characteristic over-generosity he declares in the programme notes: 'In our own times the outstanding vehicle of musical progress has been the Cyril Scott Piano Sonata, Op.66, with its irregular rhythms (originally an Australian invention), its 'non-architectural' flowing form, its exquisitely discordant harmonies. The Scott Sonata is as significant artistically, emotionally and pianistically as it is historically . . .' In this panegyric, however, he omits to mention that it was he himself who first gave me the idea of writing in irregular rhythms.

Like many notabilities, Grainger has his peculiar hobbies and tastes, as witness the naïve colloquialisms, such as 'louden lots', 'hold till blown' etc. to be found in his scores. Yet even these only give the slightest idea of his numerous idiosyncrasies.

When I first met him, and his mother, in Frankfurt – he was then only thirteen – I thought that his extravagant notions and fantastic projects were just boyish dreams that would vanish with maturity. But not at all; he still holds to the opinions he expressed in his 'teens and will vehemently argue in support of them. One of his curious dicta is that no democrat should write a concerto, for all concertos are undemocratic in principle, seeing that to the soloist is allotted a more important part than to the rest of the players!

To cap his other idiosyncrasies, Grainger has an ardent desire to revolutionize our language by getting rid of all words with foreign derivations, and as far as possible only using words of Anglo-Saxon stock. He calls his particular type of English 'Blue-eyed English', because he declares, Anglo-Saxons had blue eyes. When I have asked him why he has set himself such a Herculean task, he has replied: 'So that uncultured people may understand every word used.' But will they? Here is a sample, in which I have employed my friend's invented words, culled from his letters:

I would have joy-quaffed (enjoyed) the tonery (music) at the monk-pack-house (monastery) had the tone-tools (instruments) been more in tune with the singer-host (chorus) and the tone-smacks (accents) been in the right place. Besides, I pain-tholed (was jarred) because the middle-fiddle (viola) seemed all the time to be an othery (different) note from the wind-pipe-tone-box (organ). Nor was the tone-bill-of-fare (programme) to my liking, for most of the tone-art was of the rut-thought-full (conventional) kind, as one might fore-know (expect) when tonery is altar-slain (sacrificed) to Christ-belief (religion).

The strange thing about it all is that, whilst Grainger has such a flair for musical sound, he is apparently deaf to the sound of words and verbal jingle.

Astrologically speaking, being a Cancerian, he possesses an intense love for things of the past – though that does not preclude an interest for things of the present, for he is certainly no musical 'stickler'. He has in recent years gone to enormous trouble and expense to build and endow a museum in Melbourne, in which all the things of the past connected directly or indirectly with his own life are to be exhibited. Manuscripts, clothes, books, pictures, photographs and thousands of letters are to be housed in this 'hoard-house', as he calls it, including, to my horror, papiermâché effigies of his friends, living and dead. At first he thought to have us all there as wax figures, à la Madame Tussauds, but when I wrote and warned him that waxworks were highly inflammable (he has a phobia about fire) he modified his original idea. What upsets me, being a somewhat fastidious person, is the vulgarity of it all. A good bust or portrait is one thing, but when it comes to effigies and tailors' dummies, then my sensitive flesh begins to creep.

It may be asked how these 'images' are to be clothed? Well – some months ago I received a letter from Grainger asking me to send him old clothes I had worn forty years ago or thereabouts. 'But my dear Percy', I replied, 'surely you don't

C*

imagine that I keep my shabby old worn-out garments all that time? Not being a hoarder, I have disposed of them long since.' Whereupon he wrote suggesting that he would have a suit of clothes especially made, after the style I used to wear, and would I send him the exact measurements. Then suddenly I got an idea.

There is a tailor in the vicinity (Eastbourne) who represents a London House, and to him I went. 'Mr. Skilton', I said, 'a somewhat eccentric but famous friend of mine wants an old-fashioned suit made of doe-skin to clothe an effigy of me in a museum. He lives in America. How much do you think it would cost him over there?' 'About sixty pounds', was the answer. "And supposing you made it here in England?' 'Roughly speaking, less than half that amount.' The final upshot was that the suit was made here as depicted in an old photo, and so successfully that after wearing it a few weeks I was reluctant to part with it!

It all had its amusing side. But unfortunately these sartorial exhibits are merely a minor item, for every letter of mine that P.G. has or can get hold of is to go into his museum. He has even sent me special transparent paper on which to write or type every communication, no matter how trivial, I may address to him, the special paper being for duplication purposes in case of fire. 'And do you imagine for a moment', I have said to him, 'that anybody will want to wade through this sea of letters, many of which are not of the slightest interest?' To which he has answered, 'They will be there for reference, and so at the disposal of any musicologist or biographer who may want to prove a given point.' I fear, however, that as far as I myself am concerned I cannot share this optimism.

Enough said for the present; the reader will meet with Grainger again in the course of these *confessions*.

I have referred to the late Balfour Gardiner as another member of 'The Frankfurt Group' – a composer who in the early part of my career gave me much encouragement. To my great regret I saw little of him in later life, not because our friendship had cooled, but because he lived out of London and had become somewhat of a hermit. When I first met this lovable and original character in Frankfurt, he aroused our amusement by his slightly Oxford mannerisms and his good-natured cantankerousness, coupled with a mournful belittlement of everything he wrote. In fact this hyper-self-criticism was to be his undoing in the end, and he finally gave up music for forestry. We had all hoped, together with his teacher Iwan Knorr, that he would become a prolific composer of considerable distinction, for we were enthusiastic over the few compositions he had already produced. Instead of which, he has bequeathed to the public comparatively little to remember him by except his *Shepherd Fennel's Dance* and *A Comedy Overture*. How far indifferent health (though he *looked* robust enough) contributed to his self-dissatisfaction is difficult to say. In any case he frequently complained of what he called muddle-headedness, and declared he only felt really well in the strawberry and raspberry seasons! Yet when I suggested that if he took plenty of roughage, such as bran, with his breakfast every morning, it might have the same effect, he dismissed my suggestion as 'another of my crankish ideas'. And perhaps it was. Still, it would be a sad reflection to think that we might have had more enlivening works from this talented composer if only strawberries had fruited all the year round!

CHAPTER XV

Liverpool and Lesson-Giving

D URING the latter three years in Frankfurt I had developed some extremely unpleasant characteristics which were to cause much pain to my parents. In fact by the time I was nineteen I had become a most unbearable and arrogant young man. Having left Germany, I had returned to my parental home obsessed with the notion that Birkenhead and even Liverpool were intolerable places crowded with inartistic, brainless 'nobodies' and stuffy *bourgeois* with whom it was beneath my intellectual dignity to associate! (I lacked the perception to see that my own father was an intellectual, albeit with no knowledge of art and music).

The only bright spots for me, if so they may be called, in this imaginary desert, were Hans Lüthy and his wife who had previously converted me to Agnosticism, and two musicians then living in Birkenhead, namely Frederic Austin, subsequently to become well known in the musical world in connection with *The Beggar's Opera,* and the composer Ernest Bryson. These four individuals constituted my 'audience' as it were, for in those days no sooner had I composed something than in my enthusiasm I itched to play it to some sympathetic soul. At the time I first met Austin he was somewhat embedded in the academic rut – though he was not long to remain there – and perhaps for that very reason my fresh-from-the-Continent music intrigued him because, according to academic standards, it was slightly shocking. I remember, by the way, that both he and Bryson used to refer to it as stuff – 'Now then, let's hear your new stuff' – an irreverence which caused me to wince every time until I got used to it.

Indeed, at that period, my vanity was colossal, and something for which I had to suffer many indignities in a provincial place like Birkenhead. I had returned from Germany with 'a musician's mane' which so pained my mother that one day she said, almost in tears, 'I believe if I offered you a hundred pounds you wouldn't cut your hair'. I forget what I answered, but anyhow I was too vain and selfish to accede to her wishes. I was also too intolerant not to be annoyed at her everlasting preoccupation with 'what will people think?' 'After all,' I argued, 'parsons, naval men, soldiers and others all have their respective rig-outs to indicate their calling, so why shouldn't artists and musicians?'

Fortunately my mother soon grew accustomed to my conspicuous appearance, and no more protests came from her lips. All the same I was not to be freed from other annoyances, and I heartily cursed a clap-trap composer who had written a vocal vulgarity called *Get Your Hair Cut*, seeing that every errand-boy treated me to that offensive injunction whenever I walked along the streets.

Yet my over-long hair and the curious ties I affected were only minor aspects of my vanity, for I even considered it *infra dig.* to be seen carrying a parcel, and can actually remember saying to Mr. Lüthy – thirty years my senior! – 'Here. Carrying parcels doesn't suit my personality. Supposing you take it instead.'

This exaggerated regard for 'my personality' had largely been the result of having met while in Frankfurt the German poet Stefan George, who really *was* a personality, and for whom I had come to entertain a tremendous admiration; though unlike his many hero-worshippers I was not entirely blind to some of his failings.

Being an artist-autocrat of the most pronounced type, he roughly divided mankind into two categories; under one heading the artists and intellectuals, and under the other, the *bourgeois*, who counted as the 'nobodies'. The latter needed laws and religions to rule them and regulate their conduct, the artists ruled themselves by their aesthetic feelings and so were above laws and regulations. And this was a doctrine – fashionable among artists – which the then twenty-eight-year-old poet instilled into me and which I accepted with the same enthusiasm as I had accepted Agnosticism.

But what it did, of course, in a youth of my age, was to foster arrogance and subdue all feelings of democracy. On the other hand, one of S.G's. dicta was to stand me in good stead, in that he impressed on me that the general public was no judge of artistic values, and that no true artist must ever be swayed by either the praise or the blame of the masses. As for the critics, they were even more 'stupid' than the public, and the futility of newspaper criticism could be proved from the fact that quite frequently one review flatly contradicted another. Thus, when through string-pulling on the part of the impressive and influential poet, my First Symphony was produced at Darmstadt and greeted with mingled applause and hisses and good and bad criticisms, I was not in the least discouraged but on the whole inclined to be flattered. As to why Stefan George should have been interested in a young man over ten years his junior, this was in part due to the fact that I had set some of his poems to music in a way which, he considered, expressed the spirit of the words.

I shall, however, have more to say about this powerful and almost unique notability later on. That I came to owe him much I am the last to deny, for he was the first to awaken in me a love of poetry, which in turn had at one time a considerable influence on my music and acted for me as an inspiration. Just as the works of the novelist Jean Paul Richter had a marked effect on much of Schumann's music, and Kipling on my friend Percy Grainger's, so did the poems in particular of Ernest Dowson have their effect on my own creative efforts at the period of which I write.

All the same, my newly awakened interest in poetry was not without its humorous side, for it was partly responsible for that exaggerated preoccupation with 'my personality' which I have already mentioned. I felt I could not do this, that or the other because it was not poetic, and hence was not consistent with what I imagined ought to be 'my poetic personality'! I disliked Birkenhead – and did not even hide the fact from my parents – because I thought it was not a fitting environment either for a 'poet-composer' to have been born in or to live in; I considered I ought to dwell in some romantic, country place 'far from the madding crowd', and from which I might derive inspiration.

My attitude might well have been more philosophical had I then believed that I had shaped my present destiny as regards place of birth, parents, loves and friends, in a previous life, and that it was an unavoidable experience necessary for my evolution. But not believing that, I proved so objectionable an offspring that my parents, in despair, went to the Lüthys in the hopes of finding some means of dealing with my deplorable traits. In an effort to pacify their quite excusably hurt and troubled minds, Mr. Lüthy adopted the attitude: 'Well, well – you must remember that your son is a genius (?) and one has to make allowances. Geniuses aren't like ordinary people, and you can't expect them to behave as such. It is probably only a difficult phase he is going through, and will pass. My advice to you is to try and be more understanding . . . Of course, if the worst comes to the worst, you know where Cyril will find a home.'

Meanwhile, despite these crises, I was dividing my time between composing and practising hard at the piano, the plan being that I should give a recital in Liverpool, and then settle down there to give lessons to such pupils as I could obtain. And here my vanity intruded again. My complete array of names being Cyril Meir Scott, I thought it would sound more imposing to have myself billed as C. Meir-Scott; and what is more, I stuck to my resolve in spite of protests from my parents and Mr. Lüthy. One minor reason for this silly juggling with my name was that, strange to say, there happened to be an organist in Birkenhead named Cyril Scott, and I did not wish to be confounded with this worthy individual, my respect for organists not being of the highest.

It says much for the kindness of my parents' acquaintances, including the imposing Canon Robson, that many of them took tickets for my debut, and as for the Lüthys, they contrived to lure a gratifying number of Liverpudlians into the hall.

Yet although the venture was a success, the papers were kind, and my father was left with no bill to foot, it only brought me two pupils at half-a-guinea a lesson, and a benevolent elderly bachelor who paid me the same sum to play Bach to him once a week. I can still, by the way, remember a quaint remark made by Mr. Lüthy about this 'Bach-fan', namely; 'Mr. Hall is really quite an intelligent man, but he gives himself in such a silly way.' My Swiss friend's English was not invariably idiomatic.

My pupils insisted on paying my fee after each lesson – and how embarrassed I felt at taking the money! Indeed, all through my adult life I have hated anything to do with pecuniary transactions. Equally have I hated 'peddling my wares' and thrusting my works under conductors' noses; so much so that only after hard self-driving could I bring myself to display such forwardness. Many times have I been rebuked for this cowardice, laziness, diffidence or whatever it may be – yet I remain incorrigible, the commercial instinct and the creative urge not being twins that find a place in my particular make-up. This is not to say that where business is concerned I would allow myself to be taken advantage of, nor when I say that for me the most worth-while things are those having nothing to do with money, I therefore look down on commerce and on business men as inferior beings. Far from it. . . . But I have digressed, and must get on with my story. . .

For living and teaching purposes my mother found me some rooms, which looked promising enough but did not prove so in the end. It was the usual story, the landlady, so she said, had known better days, had never wanted to let rooms but would 'do everything to make the young gentleman comfortable'. One stipulation we made was that no piano was to be played in the house unless I was out, for I could not possibly compose against musical noises. For meals, except breakfast, I would be going to the University College Club, as it then was, and of which I was to become a member.

And yet, so much for promises! No sooner had a few months elapsed than my landlady, a dismal, sallow woman, took in a foreigner *en famille*, who proceeded to play the piano in the very next room whenever he felt inclined. To add to my troubles I was tormented by barrel-organs, the grinders of which, when I angrily shouted at them to depart, would merely smile ingratiatingly and refuse to budge, or simply move a few paces further off but not out of earshot. Obviously Canning Street was no place for a composer, nor as far as I could see was any street in benighted Liverpool!

Even so, despite the organ-grinders and other annoyances, I did manage to compose at least one lengthy and pretentious work, a *Piano Concerto*. There was a French Canadian music enthusiast with whom Paderewski always stayed when he visited Liverpool, and in my youthful conceit and enthusiasm I had *hoped* that through her kind offices the renowned pianist might be induced to look at the work and subsequently to play it. Needless to say, my hopes were never realised, nor indeed might they have been even if the work had been worthy of a performance and not the completely immature effort it actually was. Apart from other considerations, what in my innocence I did not realise in those days was that even great artists cannot just play anything they like, for it is their managers or the concert promoters who dictate what they shall or shall not play. It seems unnecessary to add that I have long since consigned the Concerto to the dustheap. . . In later years I was to meet Paderewski several times – on one occasion at Lady Randolph Churchill's – and he was always charming, asked me to play some of my piano pieces, and invited me to visit him at his estate on Lake Geneva.

My stay in Liverpool, dislike the place as I then did, was to prove an ultimate blessing. For at the University Club I made a contact among others which was to have far-reaching results both morally and artistically. It was with Dr. Charles Bonnier, a Frenchman, at that time professor of French literature at the University College.

In *My Years of Indiscretion* I erroneously gave his age as about forty-seven at the time, but have since remembered that he was only thirty-nine, though being stoutish, bearded and bespectacled he appeared much older. If reincarnation did not explain the forming of what might seem strange friendships, it would remain a mystery to me why this much older man should for a few years have linked his life with an immature and opinionated young upstart like myself. Yet, nonetheless, we rented a small house together, and there we lived until for reasons mostly connected with my career I moved to London, which became my permanent place of abode until 1939.

It is said that, with few exceptions, two members of the female sex cannot live together without quarrelling, but if that is true, all I can say is that they are less fortunately constituted than we males. For I can look back on the time I spent with Charles Bonnier as one of complete, uplifting and stimulating harmoniousness. Indeed, my association with him went far to proving the occult truth that humans, whether they realise it or not, are affected by each other's magnetism – in a word, by their auras – and that is one reason for the yogic injunction, 'keep good company'.

Bonnier was a man of such noble and selfless character that, without seeming to do so, he influenced me for good in a way that I believe no other mortal could have done at that unpleasant stage of my life. By which I do not mean of course that he turned me into anything approaching a saint, for he was no thaumaturgist, but he did help me to shed my ridiculous arrogance to adopt a more democratic outlook. . . . On the surface he seemed to be incongruously versatile; he wrote poetry, prose philosophy, belles-lettres, articles on socialism (of the French type) and he painted pictures in the *pointilliste* style. But the strangest of all his activities was connected with his intense love of Wagner. In a loud tenor voice he would sing stretches of the Wagnerian operas, the while he would accompany himself on – of all things – a harmonium! (Not when I was trying to compose, of course). This instrument reposed incongruously in his own sitting-room, on the walls of which he had hung enormous French posters by Toulouse Lautrec of ballet-dancers, or maybe they were prostitutes, displaying a large expanse of leg and white drawers.

In striking contrast to this *demi-mondaine* atmosphere was our joint living and dining room, which, although neither of us believed in the Christian religion as such, we had tried to make look as much like a monk's cell as our purses and inventive powers permitted. Why? – because the external aspects of ecclesiasticism appealed to us as something poetic and flavouring of a romantic past. To produce the monastic effect, we had blocked up the lower half of the window and installed gothic-shaped, leaded-light windows in the upper half. As for furniture, it consisted of a table, a dresser, a long church-looking bench, and two kitchen arm-chairs of the Windsor variety. Nothing could have been harder and more uncomfortable – though Bonnier being fat suffered less than I did – yet what was lacking in comfort was, as we thought, made up for by 'atmosphere'.

Anyway, in these curious surroundings my companion taught me the technique of versification which, apart from enabling me to translate a number of Baudelaire's poems and some of Stefan George's, was to become invaluable to me when I came to write my opera-libretti many years afterwards. Besides which, under benign influence of the ever cheerful, philosophical yet amusingly 'bitter and gay' Dr. Charles, my disgraceful attitude towards my ill-used parents had materially changed for the better, and in consequence they had come to take a more favourable view of their black sheep of a son.

Although in my youthful arrogance I spoke disparagingly of Liverpool, I nonetheless made some interesting friends there. Among them was the late George Hall Neale, who subsequently became a very distinguished portrait-painter. Some thirty years after our first meeting, when we had both moved to London, and my musical reputation – such as it had become – was at its height, he invited me to sit for him. After his death, the Committee of the National Portrait Gallery asked his widow to bequeath the picture to that Institution, with a view to hanging it after my own death . . . Of Hall Neale, lovable, modest man that he was, it can rightly be said that, unlike many otherwise fine artists, he obtained absolutely 'speaking likenesses' of his large number of sitters.

CHAPTER XVI

First Performances of my Earliest Works

I must now pick up, so to say, some of the dropped stitches of my story. Young people being apt to be pretentious, I had, as already mentioned, been daring enough while still a student to compose a Symphony. Whether it would ever have been performed had not my poet-friend Stefan George known Herr Willem de Haan, the conductor of the Opera-House at Darmstadt, is a very doubtful question. Anyway, through the united good graces of these two *Herren*, it *was* performed, and as I have said, was received with mingled applause and hisses. Even so, Herr de Haan and his attractive daughter were to become good friends to me, and I can still recall a fragment of a letter he wrote in English, in which he quaintly said: 'I hope you will pay us to and fro a visit to Darmstadt, and bring us by that occasion such nice composition as till now'!

Nevertheless when some years later I 'brought him' my *Piano Sonata* (No. 1), which ends with a fugue, he found the work much too discordant for his taste and objected to its irregular rhythms. Shaking his head in disapproval, he said: 'No! I cannot like the rest of the Sonata. But the fugue – that is a masterpiece!'

I have no memory for dates, I only know that the Symphony was produced during the Boer-war period when we English were very unpopular in Germany; indeed Balfour Gardiner told me that he had overheard one irate member of the audience say: 'They should play that to the Boers, and then they would run to the Equator!' Incidentally, some months before the performance, when I was still living at Oxton, my mother informed me that she had met a acquaintance, who naïvely observed: 'I saw your son this morning walking along. He seemed very pensive.

I suppose he was thinking of his piece (!) which is going to be performed at Darmstadt.'

Yet, as it so happened, I was by then preoccupied with 'pieces' even more pretentious than the Symphony, one being a lengthy choral work, which I am glad to say has never been performed. Among other works, I had written a Piano Quartet, an effort subsequently to place me in a conspicuous manner before the British public, though today I consider the work unrepresentative and old-fashioned and wish it had not been published. But at least it provides evidence to refute the assumption that I have remained exactly where I began, namely in a state of complete stagnation. Even so, Sir Charles Villiers Standford, then at the apex of his career, thought the work a bit too unrestrained, yet conceded that I had talent. He altered his opinion, however, when a few years later I had become still more unrestrained and had 'progressed'. He then anathematized me as a 'lost soul', and pronounced some songs of mine as 'simply blasphemous!' What he would have thought of present-day music is beyond conjecture.

Amateurs who imagine that the first performance of an orchestral work is all joy for a composer are sadly mistaken. All sorts of untoward things may happen, and did happen regarding my Symphony. When I arrived in Frankfurt the day before the first rehearsal, it was to find that the fellow who was to have copied all the parts had failed me badly. In consequence I and the ever willing and enthusiastic Grainger were faced with having to sit up all night copying the wretched things at full speed. This irksome task completed, we had to catch an early train to Darmstadt. The arrangement was that Herr de Haan should take the first rehearsal, and I was to conduct the second one the following day and the performance itself.

I had assumed that to conduct a work of one's own would be little short of child's-play. But I had only waved the baton for a few moments when I discovered to my dismay that I could no more direct an orchestra than I could sprout wings. 'Gentlemen,' I said, 'it is no good – I can't conduct,' and with that I descended from the rostrum and appealed to Herr de Haan.

I may mention here that generally speaking it is as much an illusion to imagine that composers should be good conductors as that conductors should be good composers, for conductor-ship requires many qualities in which scores of creative artists are entirely lacking. Although I subsequently learnt enough not to repeat the Darmstadt-fiasco, I have always preferred to leave my works to experienced conductors to grapple with rather than conduct them myself – if not disastrously, at any rate indifferently.

How much prestige the Symphony-performance gave me is difficult to say. Certainly Mr. Lüthy, who had travelled all the way to Germany to hear it, made the most of the incident to boost my name in Liverpool, in particular with members of the Liverpool Philharmonic Committee. I remember that on my return to England he brought me into contact with one old gentleman of that body, who had a pronounced squint and who persisted in calling me and referring to me as 'Mr. Myer' – my *karma* for calling myself C. Meir-Scott! This askew-eyed person-age was induced by my enthusiastic and persuasive patron to give me an introduction to Frederic Cowen, later knighted, who then conducted the Liverpool Philharmonic, and on whom I eventually called, at his house in London, where I played to him on a small and atrocious upright piano an Overture for one of Maeterlinck's plays I had recently composed. (The Overture had already been performed at one of the Palmengarten Concerts in Frankfurt.) My interview with Cowen, however, bore no fruit as far as Liverpool was concerned; and come to that, unless I am much mistaken, the only orchestral works of mine ever to have been performed in that city are the *Heroic Suite* (since discarded), which the notable Dr. Hans Richter produced, and my *Two Passacaglias* which Albert Coates con-ducted there, some time during the 'thirties. (Although this latter work has always scored a success when given a hearing, performances of it are nonetheless very rare occurrences. But then, strangely enough, success seems to have little to do with programme-compiling.)

With regard to the *Heroic Suite* – my second lengthy orchestral work after the Symphony – it had been a long and roundabout business to get at Richter, and had it not been for the indefatigable string-pulling activities of Mr. Lüthy, the interview would never have been achieved.

This great conductor, who had been the first to conduct Wagner's *Ring* at Bayreuth, was one of those fat, thick-necked, grunting, square-bearded, gauche, professional types who do nothing to set one at one's ease, but give the impression that the whole business of meeting one is a dreadful bore. I had gone out to Bowdon, near Manchester, where he was living at the time, and having been shown into his music room, I waited some time for him to appear. It was a showery afternoon, and when he finally did appear in a loose jaeger suit, of which he had not even buttoned the trousers, he grunted something about having been out and got wet. I felt anything but comfortable inside myself, and I fervently wished that he could have been a little more gracious as he opened the piano and indicated that I should proceed. Nevertheless, by the end of my performance, his grunts had given way to, for me, very gratifying expressions of enthusiasm, the upshot being that he promised to produce the work both in Manchester and Liverpool – a promise which he faithfully kept.

Yet to pronounce the Suite 'a fine and original work', as he had done, was to become in my opinion a gross overstatement. On the other hand, it was going too far in the other direction to say, as did one of the Liverpool critics, that the work as it stood was 'not worth the serious attention of the conductor, the orchestra or the audience'. Not only was that verdict in the opinion of many musicians entirely unjust, but it was an insult to 'the great Richter', and implied that he had no musical judgment at all. For was it not Richter who really 'made' Elgar, having assessed the value of his *Enigma Variations?*

My own view about Richter's opinion of the *Suite* is simply
that it appealed to him because it was outside the rut of those
academic compositions which, especially in England, were
being produced at that period. Satisfactory as regards form
and orchestration, it had just that amount of unusualness, and
no more, which he at his age and at that time demanded
from a new work. Even so, with all due respect for the opinion
of so eminent a man, it soon came to displease me because it
had ceased to be representative of my musical aims and ideas,
one of the latter being that if a creative artist is to be remembered at all, he should be remembered by his best works
and not by his youthful indiscretions.

However, I must not pursue this line of thought, but must
mention the chamber-music venture which first brought me
into the London limelight. It was my fellow-composer, Roger
Quilter, who indirectly brought this about. He had a friend
who was associated with the well-known firm of John Broadwood & Sons, and if I remember rightly it was this obliging
young man who introduced me to Mr. W. H. Leslie, the first
Chairman of Lloyd's Brokers Association and also a Director
of the House of Broadwood. In order to further the sales of
Broadwood pianos, Mr. Leslie conceived the idea of giving a
series of chamber-music concerts in St. James Hall, since
demolished, and among other artists he had in view was
Kreisler. He wanted Kreisler to appear in concerted music,
as it is loosely called, and moreover actually to play the
violin part in my *Piano Quartet*. I had given the broad-minded
Mr. Leslie, who had done much for choral music, a sketchy
but doubtless impassioned performance of the work as best I
could on the piano, and evidently he was so impressed that
'he took me up', so to say, a part of his benevolent activities
being to introduce me to several music-loving grandees.
Thus he brought about my first introduction to London high
life, as a useful step, so he thought, to musical fame!

But the burning question at the moment was whether
Kreisler would consent to play in the work of an unknown

young Englishman? Fortunately for me, and my own reputation, he did consent after I had played the work through to
him, *and* his wife (very important, as Mr. Leslie said) on one
memorable morning when, judging from their attire, both my
listeners had just risen from their bed.

The ensuing concert brought my name before the public in a
manner which, short of murder, nothing else could have done.
Reviews of the *Piano Quartet* appeared in all the papers, including *The Church Times* – and thus before my mid-twenties I
had been launched on the uncertain waters of my career! . . .
Years later, I may add, Kreisler made a violin arrangement
of my piano piece *Lotusland*, and played it during an extensive
tour in China and Japan, where it proved such a success, so
he informed the *Sunday Times*, that on occasions he had to
repeat it three times. Personally I must confess that I prefer
his violin arrangement of my piece to the original piano
version, and think that had I not been discouraged by my
publisher from writing violin pieces, I would probably have
conceived it for that instrument in the first place.

CHAPTER XVII

How I Gained my Undesired Reputation

BY the time of which I have just written, Percy Grainger and his mother had left Frankfurt and were living in London, the intention being that Grainger should embark on his career as a pianist, composition affording no adequate means of a livelihood.

Mrs. Grainger was an extremely attractive blonde; a self-sacrificing, wise-minded woman with an unusually good head for business, whom I shall always remember with great affection, for she treated me almost like a second son until her tragic death in 1921.

Grainger had already produced some remarkable numbers, including a few of those choral items for which he has since become so well known. He was at the time of which I write a somewhat Shelleyesque-looking young man with very fine features and a shock of light golden hair; a *tout ensemble* which aroused the amorous emotions of susceptible young women. And not only *young* women, for there was one woman, who must have been well in her late forties, about whom my friend will doubtless have much to say when he comes to write his own life-story in his 'blue-eyed' English. Suffice it here to mention that I indirectly benefited by the passion which this society woman, a Mrs. L—, conceived for Grainger, for seeing that I was so close a friend of his, she not only invited me several times to stay in her house but also introduced me to a number of influential people. She believed in the occult, by the way, a subject which in those days I treated with the contempt born of ignorance, though I was diplomatic enough to feign assent to the various extravagant statements she made.

In order to make propaganda for Grainger, Mrs. L. gave

'evenings' at her large house overlooking the Thames, to which people with singing voices (and some who had none) would be invited for the purpose of performing his choruses. Among those invited were Quilter and Balfour Gardiner, who declared that he couldn't sing in any choral works unless he stopped up his ears so as not to be deflected from his own part by the part his neighbour was singing. In consequence he cut rather a humorous figure, shouting away with his hands clapped to the sides of his head.

It was at one of these musical parties that I first met Gervase Elwes, that fervent Roman Catholic convert who, after being in the British diplomatic service for a few years, began his career as a singer at the age of thirty-seven. I remember that he astonished us all by telling us that he was already the father of a large family – a confession which set me wondering why on earth any man, especially an artist, should want to burden himself with such a host of children, or with any at all for that matter. But I did not realise then that Catholics hold some curious views about depriving God of souls.

During the next fifteen years or so I was often to meet this artistic singer and charming man. Yet although he professed an admiration for my songs and for my status as a musician, he never to my knowledge sang a single one of them – at any rate in public. The last I saw of him was in New York at a time when in 1921 we both happened to be touring America, and where he met with his tragic death three days after our meeting. The news of the accident – he fell between a train and the platform – came in a letter from Mrs. Grainger when I was concertising in Winnipeg, and naturally was a great shock to me, as it was equally to Grainger and herself, with their outstanding capacity for friendship. For many years a bust of Gervase Elwes reposed in the Queen's Hall, before the latter's destruction in the blitz.

Around the time of Grainger's peculiar romance with Mrs. L—, I had composed a bravura piece which I called *An English Waltz*. Meanwhile my friend had secured an engagement to tour with that very much passé celebrity Adelina Patti who,

although she retained her artistry had only the last remnants
of a voice. Her refusal to rest on her laurels, however, was to
bring both Grainger and myself some good luck, for he played,
with success, my showy piece in a large number of towns and
thereby brought my name – such as it was – increasingly before
the public, and at the same time made people realise that he
was a remarkable pianist.

Even so there is something unaccountable about what
executants will do or take up. Whereas the success of my Waltz
did not tempt a number of pianists to perform it, no sooner had
I written my *Blackbird's Song* and my *Lullabye*, and of piano
pieces my *Danse Negre* and my *Waterwagtail* than these trifles
were to find a place in scores of programmes. Much the same
must be said about the *Two Pierrot Pieces*, which I wrote in
Liverpool before my mid-twenties. Indeed, the success of these
small pieces did me both good and harm, in that on the one
hand they made my reputation and on the other they killed my
reputation as a composer of larger and more serious works, as,
for instance, did Schubert's songs during his lifetime.

There was another thing relative to larger works which
certainly did not prove helpful, namely the insistent desire to
have 'first performances' of British compositions, leaving what
might happen to them afterwards in the lap of the gods, who
apparently were not at all interested. This insistence on first
performances even became a standing joke among musicians,
one waggish notability being moved to remark that the Albert
Hall (because of its echo) was the only hall in which a British
composer could hear his work *twice!*

Be that as humorists would like to have it, a second Symphony
I wrote in my twenties and which Sir Henry Wood produced at
The Proms, never, despite its success, got a second hearing;
though some years later, after I had chosen to reduce it to *Three
Orchestral Danses*, I did conduct it in Birmingham at the request
of the late Sir Landon Ronald. Apropos that second Symphony,
I remember Baron Frederic d'Erlanger (composer of operas and
other works) introducing himself to me after the performance,

in order, as he said, to express his admiration for my mastery of orchestral colouring. Perhaps it behoves me to add that he was a polite Frenchman. Anyhow, compliment or sincerity on his part, my own opinion is that I did not write a (to me) satisfying orchestral work till around 1912, when I composed my *Two Passacaglias*, which, unless my memory errs, were first produced by the Royal Philharmonic Society.

Meanwhile, amongst others, I had written my *Piano Quintet* (it subsequently won the Carnegie Award) which I considered a marked advance on the chamber work in which Kreisler had played. This work received its first hearing privately at the *salon* of Miss Evelyn Suart, as prior to her marriage, she then was. I had met this talented pianist at the Graingers, the outcome being that she invited me to her home, where she and her mother kept open house for musicians and other types of artists.

Miss Suart was an original and highly vivacious young lady who took a delight in the unusual or anything more or less calculated to 'dumbfound the burghers' as the French phrase goes; and both she and her mother soon came to believe in me and to champion my 'cause'. They invited me to stay at their flat, with its large music-room, whenever I came to London; and, being a susceptible young man, I soon fell for the charms of my engaging propagandist. But, like most artists, she was temperamental and apt to be touchy at times, and there were tiffs now and then, not only with me but with her mother. It all had its amusing side, for after a tiff with me she would unburden herself to her mother and after a tiff with her mother she would unburden herself to me, who could hardly take sides against my very hospitable hostess! Altogether, what with two temperamental young people to cope with – and doubtless I was the worse offender – poor Mrs. Suart was landed in no enviable position. It says much for her patience and good nature that instead of bidding me begone she still offered her *salon* for my contention-arousing music.

And it certainly did arouse contention. After the first per- formance of the *Piano Quintet*, so I was told, people had stood in groups arguing violently for or against, some praising me and others denouncing 'this twenty-five-year-old debaser of musical morals with his extravagant and discordant effusions'! As for the professors, it took many years before even my now considered mild and inoffensive songs and piano pieces were taught in any of the reputable music institutions.

Yet meanwhile, despite this hostility, I had contrived, partly through the critic Robin Legge, and partly through the kindness of Mr. W. H. Leslie, to find more than one publisher. By dint of paying the bill, Mr. Leslie had induced Messrs. Boosey & Co. to publish my *Piano Quintet*, in consideration of which they were also prepared to publish some of my smaller pieces. But as it later transpired, the firm of Boosey was not the right sort of publishers for me, seeing that in those days they were chiefly interested in what were erroneously called 'ballads'; a type of nauseatingly sentimental song of little or no musical value at all. To further these deplorable indications of English bad taste as it then was, whole concerts (called Ballad Concerts) of them were given, during which one singer after another sailed, tripped or glided on to the platform to delight the entirely unmusical audience with the cloying banalities they were well paid to sing. By way, however, of incidental relief to these *concerts de levres*, an instrumentalist would be engaged, and on one occasion I was that instrumentalist as composer-cum-interpreter of my *Two Pierrot Pieces* (a Boosey publication). Mr. Arthur Boosey had even hoped to find in me a lucrative proposition when he decided to interest himself in my non-balladesque type of song, and so for a short while had paid me a retaining fee, an arrangement which suited me very well. But as his hopes were not realised with the speediness he desired, one day he informed me with a doleful face that I had proved a commercial disappointment, and as there was no real contract between us I must consider the arrangement at an end.

It was then that Miss Suart stepped into the breach and introduced me to the late Mr. William Elkin who had just founded the firm of Messrs. Elkin & Co., with which I have had my long and harmonious association over all the years.

Much can be said for the courage of Mr. Elkin senior that he took up a young man who defied the academic traditions and whose adversaries, the teachers and professors, were in far more advantageous positions than were his friends. The whole business meant a long and uphill struggle. Yet my enterprising publisher was to win through in the end; though the policy he adopted to gain that end had certain drawbacks so far as I was concerned. He had stipulated that I should write a certain number of piano-pieces and songs every year, with the result that I composed far too many, and seeing that they deflected attention from my more serious works, I have little doubt that they contributed to my undoing. As to whether I shall live them down when I have ceased to live in my present guilty 'garment of the soul', is a matter about which I would not venture to prophesy. In fact it would be immodest and presumptuous to do so, for it would imply that I think my works worthy to endure after I, their creator, have departed to other Planes.

Which reminds me of a story told to me by Mr. S. Goldwyn, the film magnate, whom I met some years ago at a party. There was a young woman present who kept pestering me to play one of my piano-pieces. 'But people want to talk, not to hear me play,' I objected, and so I firmly refused. Finally she went up to Goldwyn and said; 'Mr. Scott won't play to us. Don't you think it very unkind of him?' 'On the contrary,' was the answer, 'I admire him for it. Would you have him like Gershwin, who can never be dragged away from the piano? I was talking to the fellow only the other day, and he asked me: "Do you think my compositions will still live in a hundred years' time?" "They most certainly will," I said, "if *you* are still here to play them".'

CHAPTER XVIII

Literary Friends, and Days in Shere

DURING the year of my association with Dr. Bonnier in Liverpool, we decided to spend part of one of the summer holidays in Ambleteuse, that little seaside place not far from Dieppe. It was there that I met Mrs. Robert Alan Stevenson, cousin by marriage to Robert Louis Stevenson. Robert Alan and Robert Louis, besides being cousins, had been very close friends, and she told me that they had talked over many of the plots of the latter's books.

R.A. himself had been an art critic, having written a very fine book on Botticelli. As a man, he had held what many people would regard as highly peculiar views on marriage, for he did not believe in any form of conjugal jealousy – views shared by his wife; though I never thought to ask her whether she had believed in them *prior* to their marriage. In any case, living together on entirely non-jealous lines, she and her husband had been the perfect comrades, and so united a couple that they could confide in each other their *affairs* without the least apprehension on either side of disrupting their unity. 'After all,' Mrs. Stevenson said to me, 'what is jealousy but a selfish, childish and ignoble emotion? For two people to feel jealous after they have once got over the illusory in-love stage is simply vanity.' Besides which, she impressed on me, conjugal jealousy is largely a convention evolved by man to gratify his sense of possession – 'If I marry a woman, she belongs to me' sort of thing! And the result in hundreds of cases is simply deception; men deceive their wives and women their husbands. In some ways the conjugal-jealousy-convention is worse for the men than for the women, for men are polygamous by nature whilst women are more apt to be 'clingers'. Another thing is that women grow old-looking sooner than men, or they may get fat; and some men hate fat women from the sexual point of view. So instead of the conjugal-jealousy idea making for lasting marriages, it makes for divorce, and misconduct, as they call it, is the excuse put forward to get it through.

These were the doctrines that the widowed Mrs. Stevenson instilled into my mind as we went for walks by the sea, and which I accepted with the same enthusiasm as I had accepted Agnosticism. I must have been about twenty-three at the time. Mrs. Stevenson also impressed on me that mere in-loveness was no wise basis for a happy marriage, and that one only really got to know a woman after one had ceased to be in love with her.

Mrs. S. had her two children with her, to whom she always referred as 'my offspring', one being a young boy of about nine and the other a very beautiful girl around twenty, for whom I proceeded to conceive a deeply romantic passion. Although Mrs. S. realised that the affair could not lead to marriage, true to her principles she helped me in every way, and after we left Ambleteuse, invited me to stay with them in Chiswick whenever I came to London. (In fact I was staying with the Stevensons at the time of my debut with Kreisler in the St. James' Hall).

Since those days in Ambleteuse I have met many and varied personalities, and yet I look back on Mrs. Stevenson as being almost unique, considering the stuffy and conventional times in which she lived. She was a most entertaining conversationalist, had known a number of notabilities, including Oscar Wilde, and as for matters of sex, she displayed a tolerance towards them worthy of a psycho-analyst, long before the name of Freud had ever been heard. She had her roguish side too, for although an agnostic, she told me, much to my amusement, that at one time she had made 'pin money' by writing goody-goody stories for religious or semi-religious magazines, as also religio-sentimental verses for Christmas cards. And with it all, she fulminated against the 'frightful humbug and hypocrisy' of the age in which she lived. But not so her daughter, who far from taking after either of her parents, loved everything that was conventional, so that she had nothing in common with her emancipated mother, nor yet, incidentally with me. Thus, our romance in the end suffered the fate of many of its kind, and in consequence of not seeing her any more, I lost touch with that remarkable soul, her mother.

Nevertheless, before we parted, Mrs. S. brought me into contact with the novelist H. B. Marriott-Watson and his poetess-wife Rosamond, many of whose verses I subsequently set to music. Marriott-Watson was a massive man, Australian born, who, what with his shock of untidy hair, big moustache, sunny smile and thick lips, struck me as being somewhat like an Italian organ-grinder. As for his wife, she was a tall, stately and over-stout woman with a charming intonation and a delightful way of speaking. Mrs. Stevenson and this impressive couple were very great friends; but Mrs. S. had made the mistake of talking to them in a too laudatory manner about me, and in consequence they had taken a theoretical dislike to me before we actually met. However, as soon as the meeting was brought about, they entirely altered their attitude, which was fortunate for me, seeing that the more literary people I consorted with the better for my allround education. Moreover, I was destined to enjoy a warm friendship with them until the poetess died some years later, and her husband's over-indulgence in stimulants made association with him too embarrassing.

Meanwhile, Marriott, as I came to call him, had lunched me several times at the Savile Club and introduced me to various notabilities he thought might be interested and helpful. But the introduction for which I came to be most grateful was not to an individual but to a place, namely the picturesque and poetic village of Shere, near Guildford, where he and his wife took up their abode and where they remained for the rest of their lives. To this charming village I made frequent and prolonged visits, stayed in rooms, and did much creative work. It was there that I wrote *Lotusland*, and, I think, *Vesperale;* a piece for which I have little liking, though I shed tears when in the 'thirties it was played at the Memorial Service for Mr. Elkin senior, he himself having been especially fond of it. To add some romantic colour to the piece for imaginative persons, a story went round that I had composed it sitting on a gravestone in Shere church-yard; but, if so, I have no recollection of the lugubrious fact.

In Shere and its surroundings I had at last found in England the environment I felt was appropriate to a poet-musician – in a word, to my personality! There I could see, or rather, feel myself 'alone and palely loitering' on the Surrey hills, and dreaming my ambitious musical dreams. And when I wanted company I could go and sit with Rosamond in her charming garden (she wrote a poetic book on gardens) or play to her my latest composition, or have a chuckle over recent local happen-ings. Nor I fear was our conversation always on a very high level, for with all her stately dignity and refinement, this minor poetess had an almost schoolgirl taste for the ribald, and for matters not politely mentionable in drawing-rooms. Sometimes amusing things would happen to her. She had a rather peculiar handwriting. Why she should have written all the way to London for a small *cucumber*, I cannot think. But anyhow, one day a mysterious parcel arrived containing, not that vegetable, but a very diminutive *pot de chambre*.

Apart from the *Lullabye*, my two most popular songs, *The Blackbird's Song* and *The Unforeseen* were composed to her verses. Although I wrote the former in Chelsea, where I had taken rooms after leaving Liverpool, when we discussed it in Shere we found it was too short, so Rosamond obligingly wrote an extra verse for it. She herself was delighted with the setting, but I have always borne a grudge against the song, for I had merely to be introduced to this or that gushing woman for her to say; 'So you are the composer of the lovely *Blackbird's Song?*' – a remark that made me wince every time. Not knowing what to reply, sometimes I merely bowed and said nothing, or else I commented on their very bad taste. . . .One may ask, then, how I came to write it in the first place? The answer is that I wrote it at a time when I was suffering from painful pricks of conscience because I had not fulfilled my duty to the good Mr. Elkin, having long kept him waiting for an item to publish. Thus, although destitute of any real inspiration, I forced myself to write the later to become hackneyed song; a fact, I grant, hardly worth relating were it not another example of the tricks fate can play with many an ill-starred composer.

I have previously mentioned that at the time of writing, Percy Grainger is playing my *Piano Sonata No. 1* to American audiences. This was my first (for me) important piano work, and most of it was composed in Shere while I was sharing rooms with an intimate friend, to whom I may only refer as J.B. As Mr. Elkin did not wish to publish such a difficult, 'discordant' and unsaleable work without some financial assistance, this generous friend paid for the engraving. The *Sonata* was subsequently taken up and played by several notable pianists on the Continent, but to my knowledge, has never been paid an equal compliment in England.

My frequent visits to Shere came to an end about 1909, some two years before Rosamond Marriott-Watson died of a lingering and painful illness. A curious incident happened shortly after her death.

When I first met her and Marriott, we were all three agnostics. Then, during the ensuing years, I became interested in Yoga and the immortality of the soul, about which with youthful but indiscreet enthusiasm I would hold forth to them when I ought to have kept silent. And of course the effect was merely to bore them and arouse their antagonism, not to me, but to the subject itself. Then, one day, to my intense astonishment, owing to some book they had read, they both became the most convinced and dogmatic spiritualists. I say dogmatic advisedly, because although Occultism embraces Spiritualism as at any rate one aspect of immortality, they would have none of it, and would only accept the spiritualistic viewpoint as the '*Whole* Truth'.

They had a domestic who had been nurse to their only son, and whom they had retained after he had become a youth; and from what I gathered from J.B. she may have had some mediumistic powers which might have been drawn upon. In any case, very shortly after Rosamond had passed over, the following discovery was made – the door of the W.C. was locked on the inside, and there was nobody within to have locked it. Nor could anyone have got in through the window, for it was bolted. It was, to say the least, very mysterious, and Marriott, for his comfort, was absolutely convinced that his wife had somehow contrived to perpetrate this joke as a sign from the spirit world.

Marriott survived his wife for some ten years, but they were lonely and miserable ones, for he lost his son in the first world war, and thereafter he increasingly tried to derive consolation from the stupefying effects of alcohol, which hastened his death. In his younger days he had written several very readable novels, but though he had the ability to be a fine writer, his desire to live more well than wisely was his undoing, and he sacrificed his talents to the making of money, largely through journalism. He is now mostly forgotten by the reading public, but at least there is one who remembers him with affection and wishes he could have had a less tragic end.

CHAPTER XIX

The Poet Stefan George (Our First Association)

I have briefly mentioned Stefan George in a previous chapter, but considering the dramatic personality he was and the effect he had on my young life, I would be doing him a gross injustice if I were merely to let it rest at that. Indeed, so fervent an admirer am I of his poetic genius that prior to and during the second world-war I translated a large number of his poems into English verse and prefaced them with a memoir of the man himself. In this memoir I told the truth about the poet as I myself had come to know it through my personal contact with him. A few years later it was sent to a German publisher who had requested to see it with a view to having it translated and then published. But before doing so he showed the script to George's literary executor, who tried to prevent its publication on the grounds that it would defame the deceased poet.

The publisher concerned, however, was not to be deterred, so George's executor resolved and hoped to discredit my memoir by writing some very unpleasant things about me in his book *Mein Bild von Stefan George*, (Dr. Robert Boehringer). He wrote, in effect, that whereas at one time my affectionate admiration for the great poet had been evidence from letters and other material, now when I was getting old I had turned against him and had ascribed to him certain Oscar Wilde-like proclivities when he was no longer on earth to defend himself.

All this is typical of that unfortunate hero-worshipping attitude which was to prove the undoing of the Germans and was particularly pronounced among the devotees of Stefan George when he was alive, and still prevails even to-day among those special admirers of his works, who like to think of themselves as members of 'The George Circle'. In consequence most of the German books which as yet have been written about him, portray him not as a human being but as almost a sort of god, so absolutely perfect that he becomes an 'impossibility' in whom no reasonable person could believe at all. Thus, there is the legendary Stefan George and the actual Stefan George; and the latter, at any rate to English readers, is far more interesting than the former; and it was for English readers that I originally wrote the memoir, which I now have beside me so as to refresh my memory.

My first recollections of the poet date back to my student days, notably to a dark and wintry afternoon in Frankfurt when I was spending a few hours with my friend and fellow-student Baron Clemens von Franckenstein, whose brother, Sir George Franckenstein, subsequently became Austrian Minister in London before the Nazi annexation.

Although Maron Clemens – an original and charming personality – was still contending with the technique of musical composition, he had already set some of George's simpler verses, this being one reason why the poet had called on him. Moreover the two men had a friend in common in the Austrian poet and librettist Hugo von Hofmannsthal, who some years later wrote the text for Richard Strauss' opera *Der Rosenkavalier*.

The arresting feature about Stefan George was that besides being a remarkable poet he *looked* like one to a superlative degree, with pale and somewhat Dantesque face, very deep-set, rather melancholy eyes and his imposing head of long black hair, brushed back from a brow which even at twenty-eight was already furrowed. As for his manners and bearing, I can only describe them as aristocratic almost to the degree of princeliness – a matter which may have provoked André Gide's remark that, although free from conceit, he displayed 'an obvious consciousness of his obvious superiority'. This impression was doubtless created by the fact that he both loved and radiated power, though not of an agressive type, for when it suited him he could also radiate a very considerable charm; hence the influence he was later to have over his many disciples, who not only admired him but also stood in awe of him.

My first meeting with the poet was followed by others. Living as he then did at his parental home in Bingen on the Rhine, he invited Franckenstein and myself to visit him there in the spring. The outcome was that during the holidays we rode all the way on bicycles from Frankfurt to Bingen. But as Franckenstein and Norman O'Neill had become great friends, O'Neill came with us.

We put up at an hotel overlooking the Rhine, and then in the evening went round to the poet's house, who had prepared for us a large bowl of Rheinwine-cup, of which we drank till we became elated and then argumentative. Incidentally, the George family owned vineyards, and so the poet was a connoisseur of good wine. Although Norman O'Neill treated our host with respect while he was present, no sooner were we by ourselves than, as was his wont, he proceeded to treat him as a subject for mirth. As far as I remember, the two men never met again, and even meetings between Franckenstein and the poet were very infrequent. In fact, I, who happened to be the youngest of the party, was the only one destined to arouse George's special interest. Several times he came to see me in my modest rooms in Frankfurt, several times he invited me to Bingen and when, during the last months of my student days, I had moved with my effects to Cronberg in the Taunus, he came to visit me there and stayed a few days each time.

Bingen was the perfect setting, as I thought, for a great poet, with its old castle, the broad river, the long lines of vineyard-covered hills on the one side and the wooded hills on the other; and withal there was an air of melancholy about the whole place. We took many walks together, and I recall that it was during one of these rambles that Stefan George confessed that his attachment to me was no ordinary one; though he had guessed from the beginning that I was not of the type who would reciprocate his feelings. And on this score he was certainly right, for I found the confession and its cause extremely embarrassing. It is true that Franckenstein had already warned

D*

me that the poet was abnormal, and that at one time he had
been very attracted to the young Hugo von Hofmannsthal.
Even so I hardly imagined that I myself would arouse similar
sentiments, and so had not worried much about it, though I
could have wished it otherwise. Nevertheless, after the confession, I began to feel ill at ease in his presence as if a barrier
had come between us. Not that he ever attempted to win me
over to his way of thinking, nor did he ever reproach me for my
normality; yet liking and admiring him as I did, I was distressed
to think that he should have propensities which in those days
most normal people regarded with loathing and disgust.

Yet let me not be misunderstood: I believe that Stefan
George was too great an idealist to practise homosexuality in
its grossest form. On the other hand, to pretend in these days
of far greater tolerance that he was a man who merely *admired*
youths, is to display that disregard for facts which simply turns
biography into fiction. Nor must it be thought that every
admirer of the great poet's works agrees with this truth-
distorting policy. 'Everybody who knows anything about S.G.',
wrote one such admirer to me, 'knows perfectly well that he was
homosexual; the incense-swinging, adulating attempts to gloss
over a well-known constitutional fact in his personality can't
fool anyone.'

And indeed, why should it be glossed over? George could no
more help being a homosexual than, say, Chopin could help
being a consumptive; and like many homosexuals and lesbians,
he was not in the least ashamed of the fact, being almost
obsessed, as he was, with Hellenistic ideas and ideals. I remember
that on one occasion he introduced me to his fellow poet Karl
Wolfskehl as the 'young man for love of whom he could neither
eat nor sleep' – and although it was said in a somewhat light-
hearted manner, the way Wolfskehl took it showed that he knew
all about his friend's abnormality. As for myself, I felt merely
embarrassed, being still very young, (only about seventeen)
and quite unacquainted with the more unusual vagaries of
human nature. Altogether the whole situation was very complex.

If I had not admired and liked Stefan George so much, had not felt proud to be seen walking in the street or sitting in cafés with so striking and magnetic a personality, I would have somehow contrived to let the friendship cool off and so end what must have been for him a painful association. But, as it finally turned out, it was he himself who disrupted the friendship – though after a few years' separation the breach was healed and there followed a relationship which in every way was more pleasant and harmonious for both of us.

To be explicit: George had a friend named Melchior Lechter, who was a genius both as draughtsman, painter and stained-glass window designer. I first met him in company with the poet when he was passing through Frankfurt on his way back to Berlin, where he lived. He presented a most unusual exterior, which caused me to jump to the conclusion that he was a homosexual like his friend. But I was greatly mistaken, as I subsequently learnt. He had a round cherubic face with a complexion like that of a woman, very small twinkling eyes, longish light-coloured hair, and a plump physique. He dressed with great elegance but in a manner quite peculiar to himself, and he spoke with a slight lisp. At the time, his age was thirty-six. Nevertheless, in spite of the difference between our respective ages, I was soon to form a close friendship with this remarkable man, which lasted for many years. The early bond of sympathy between us was his passion for music, followed later on by the interest we both took in Occultism.

I have said that Melchior Lechter lived in Berlin; and George had impressed on me among other things that if I wanted to get myself known, I ought to visit that town and meet a number of people. He himself stayed there over a period practically every winter. Accordingly the winter (I think it was) after my symphony had been produced in Darmstadt, I made the long train journey to the German capital, and lodged for a number of weeks in a *pension*.

Lechter lived in a top flat which, apart from his studio, he had furnished almost exactly like a chapel. The furniture, of his own design, was ecclesiastical in every detail, and even his bedroom was arranged to look like a mediaeval picture. In both his rooms were beautiful stained-glass windows, which produced such a very holy atmosphere that one felt one ought never to speak above a whisper, and that to laugh would be sacrilegious. At first I was repelled by this, as I thought, inappropriate odour of sanctity in a dwelling place, but not only did I soon get used to it, but found it so poetic that it became responsible for my wish to create the same atmosphere in my *ménage* with Charles Bonnier in Liverpool.

As for Lechter himself, when I re-met him in his 'sanctuary', far from being sanctimonious, he turned out to be a most humorous individual, fond of a ribald joke, and always highly amused whenever I made a 'bloomer' in German. There was a piano in his studio on which, with his passion for music, he would induce me to play my latest compositions, parts of which he would afterwards whistle to himself, albeit in a manner which was nearly all wind and very little tone!

Possessing very catholic tastes, he was from the start much impressed by my creative efforts, immature though they were, and would invite his musician friends to hear them, believing himself, as he told me, that they had in them 'the seeds of immortality'! Whether my music helped to distract his mind from the pangs he was suffering at the time, consequent upon an unhappy love affair with an *Englishwoman*, I am not in a position to say. But he did tell both George and myself that my playing tended to soothe his lacerated spirit. He also told us both that, young as I was, being English, I might be able to throw some light on the English character; the young woman concerned having behaved in a most cruel and unaccountable way. I need hardly add that my knowledge of women, British or otherwise, being of the slightest, his hope remained mostly unrealised!

Lechter's flat was one of the meeting-places for Stefan George and his devotees at such times as he was in Berlin, and it was during one of these gatherings that the poet chose to sever our friendship. I had wandered off by myself into Lechter's bedroom to admire the sunlight streaming through the stained-glass window, when suddenly George appeared, and with an imperious gesture commanded me in one terse sentence 'never to cross his path again''. Then silencing my attempts to speak, he turned on his heel and rejoined his friends. What precisely I had done that afternoon to bring matters to this dramatic climax I was never to learn. Nor is it of any importance, not having been the basic reason for the break in our friendly relations. Neither, by the way, was the reason I gave in *My Years of Indiscretion*, published when S.G. was still alive; namely that my attitude towards him when in company with others had not always been as reverential as was right and fitting towards a man in his position. Yet even granting my guiltiness in this respect, it was he himself who had disclosed the truth about the whole unfortunate situation, when, one day as we roamed the hills near Bingen, he had said: 'Our friendship will be much easier for me when you have passed the age of twenty-three, and have shed those idealising elements which attract me in a youth'.

I forget how old I was when this confession was made; but anyway, when I *had* passed the specified age, I wrote him a long letter – which I thought was a masterpiece of diplomacy! – putting all the blame on myself, and asking him once again to take me into favour. My ostensible excuse for begging him to see me was that I wished to show him some English translations of his poems, which I thought might interest him. I informed him that I should be passing through Bingen on a certain date, and if he would be prepared to grant my request, I would break my journey there in order to visit him. If I remember rightly, I dispatched that letter from Paris, where I had been staying for some time, chiefly for the purpose of seeing Debussy and Ravel, and as it so happened, the poet received it at Lechter's flat.

Now although I had visited Berlin and seen much of Lechter during the years when George and myself had been parted, I had contrived to be discreet about the breaking of our friend-ship, for I was not certain how much Lechter knew about his friend's abnormalities. In any event, he later told me that when 'der Stefan', as we called him, got my effusion, he had thrown himself on the sofa, read it through very carefully, and having finished it, proceeded to read it through all over again. Finally he had said with evident satisfaction: 'The Scott is a crazy fellow'. This, Lechter informed me, was high praise from George! And although I merely received a postcard in reply, at least it was a favourable one.

CHAPTER XX

Stefan George (Our Second Association)

As this book is really one devoted to autobiographical confessions rather than a life-story written in chronological order, I think it best in some cases to complete my character-sketches instead of adopting the usual procedure which obtains both in history and fiction. And so I will here describe my second association with Stefan George until it finally ended around 1912 or 1913. After that year I heard nothing of him except what Melchior Lechter told me when I last saw that great artist in, I think, 1922.

During the second world war, my house was burgled no less than six times, and many papers and documents which might have thrown some light on the matter of dates were lost. Consequently I can only guess that I was twenty-four or twenty-five when I made the memorable visit to Bingen and thus renewed my friendship with the eminent poet.

It was on a very cold winter's evening that I was shown into his sanctum, where I had to wait – feeling distinctly nervous – before he appeared. When he did at last appear, instead of coming forward into the centre of the room where I was standing, he sat down very slowly on the extreme edge of a chair by the door, and making a wry face, contemplated me with an inscrutable expression. As he obviously did not propose to shake hands, I could merely, without the usual form of greeting, express my appreciation of his kindness in considering to receive me; though actually what he replied has escaped my memory. We then exchanged some remarks about the effect the years had had on our respective exteriors, and I remember that he pointed to a broad streak of white which had appeared in his leonine mane, and which he told me was due to a bereavement he had sustained in Munich. Although naturally he did not go into details at the time, I later learnt that he had lost a youth for whom he had formed so deep an attachment that the memory of him came to play an almost similar role in his imaginative life as Beatrice had done in that of Dante.

The frigid atmosphere having mellowed somewhat, I then mentioned the translations of his poems which I had brought along for him to see; and though he confessed that his brain was not very active in the evenings, he nonetheless agreed to let me read them – I do not say 'recite', because he hated his poems to be declaimed in a histrionic manner. Incidentally, he told me that one or two litterateurs had attempted renderings in English, but with such meagre success that they were almost travesties of the original.

I have mentioned earlier that whilst it was S.G. who first aroused in me a love of poetry, it was the versatile Charles Bonnier who taught me the technique of versification and encouraged me actually to write poems. In consequence, not only had I written some original verse, but, what concerns the incident, had translated several poems of Stefan George. I knew the renderings were fairly good, because Bonnier, who was a fine German scholar, had praised them. Even so, I could be far from certain whether they would please George himself. I was therefore relieved and delighted when instead of being merely interested, he became even enthusiastic about them, declaring that they were much better than any translations which had previously been attempted. Not wishing him to know before he had actually seen them that I myself was the translator, I had pretended that they were the work of someone else, and that I had merely copied them for his acceptance. But beginning to be suspicious, he wanted to hear the name of the 'poet' in question. I then hedged and lied that I would have to obtain his permission before revealing it; an excuse so palpably unconvincing that finally he said, giving me a playful slap on the cheek; 'Scoundrel! You translated them yourself!'

After this, for me, very gratifying denouement, we spent the rest of that unforgettable evening as if there had been no break in our friendship at all; my friend displaying all those stimulating and appealing qualities so characteristic of his complex and magnetic personality.

Our friendship having been re-established on a much more comfortable and secure footing, I saw him at intervals until shortly before the first world war; and I look back on the days spent with him as among the most memorable in my life. He was then at the apex of his career, had written the finest collection of his poems, *Der Siebente Ring*, and had acquired bands of admirers in several of the large German towns. And so what came to be known as 'the George circle' was formed. Its meetings were in private houses, and it was considered as a great honour to be invited. I myself was only present at one such meeting; and I still have the mental picture of 'the Master' as he allowed himself to be called, sitting at the head of a long table, at the sides of which sat a number of young males who in succession arose and read one or other of his poems in a sonorous but expressionless voice, and after a nod of approval from the master-poet, sat down again. The same performance was then repeated by another young man who had chosen a different poem. Apparently, all the gatherings of the George Circle followed more or less the same pattern; the readers were always youths or young men, and if any women were present, it was only in the capacity of 'lady waitresses' who would hand round the refreshments after the readings . . . But then, as Lechter remarked: 'Der Stefan doesn't like to have women about because they make the men amorous and so deflect the conversation from intellectual levels'!

When the passing years had brought the autumn of life to the hero-worshipped poet, it was one of disappointment and deep chargin. Although the Nazis had wanted to confer honours on him and had offered him lucrative posts, he had flatly declined them all. And no wonder; considering that they had perverted his teachings for their own political aims, and with their persuasive bombast and power to sway the people had poisoned the fruit of all his labours and aspirations, thereby rendering what he regarded as his true mission as a complete failure. And so, disgusted with Nazism and all it stood for, he left Germany for good, and died in voluntary exile at Lucano, Switzerland, in 1933.

All in all I have translated no less than 200 of George's poems. But when it came to trying to get a publisher for them I found myself again figuring as a 'bone of contention'. Whereas one publisher told me that his advisory readers regarded them as 'of the highest calibre', another publisher had virtually nothing good to say about them at all; and this despite the praise they had received from Sir Maurice Bowra, the Warden of Wadham College, Oxford, and similar praise from Dr August Closs of Bristol University, I having sent the script to both these gentlemen. Actually Sir Maurice had done me the honour of using several of my earlier translations in his impressive book *The Heritage of Symbolism*. In the letter he kindly wrote to me after reading the complete collection, he said of the translations: 'Their great virtue is that they are very *like* the originals, in shape, which is most important, in language, which is extremely difficult to get, and in temper. . . . You have managed to be both extremely faithful and yet to be poetical in the best sense.' He went on to say (what unfortunately is true) that 'modern translators don't worry at all about the form, jettison rhyme and rhythm, and dish up a sort of crib, which is very often not even trustworthy'.

But apart from this prevailing fashion to treat a poet in such a slipshod, distorting and insulting way, publishers, not unnaturally, fight shy of one they fear may be unsuited to the tastes of this beauty-fearing age. Yet whatever their fears, to suppose that vogues in tastes can ever go to prove the real merit of any poet is to suppose a fallacy; indeed what they are apt to do is to blind people to his intrinsic value. As every well-read person knows, whereas tastes and their fashions change, not so that mysterious and elusive 'something', that essence of 'poeticness' to be found in the lines of a true poet, in whichever age he may have lived. And because the best of Stefan George's poems did possess that very thing – Dr. Closs, for one, called it 'the magical quality of incantation' – I dare to predict that their final fate will not be that of un-rememberance:

Here the crossways . . .	Hands enticed you:
We are at the end.	You neared them not.
Sunk has evening . . .	Sighings choked me:
This is the end.	You heard them not?
A short ramble	Now my roadway,
Whom makes it tired?	You go it not.
Too long for me though . .	Tears are falling,
Pain makes tired.	You know it not.

(from *Der Siebente Ring*.)

CHAPTER XXI

My Introduction to Indian Philosophy

THERE are various reasons why some people change their religion, embrace new cults, adopt new creeds political and otherwise, or become believers after they have been unbelievers. In most cases they do so because they have come under the sway of some self-appointed leader, because they seek comfort after a bereavement, or because they have been glamoured by persuasive oratory, in other cases because they are dissatisfied with their present outlook and hanker after something different. Yet in my own case none of these reasons applied. I was perfectly satisfied with my Agnosticism and had no desire for any other belief – for one can believe that one *can't* know just as one can believe that one does know!

The fact is that my change of outlook came about simply through a chain of circumstances and finally through what Nietzsche called 'intellectual uprightness'. Far from wishing to believe in the immortality of mankind and the non-materialistic philosophy that goes with that doctrine, I fought against these ideas, trying to find every sort of argument to refute them, and only when I had found none that was really convincing did I eventually give in; in short, 'intellectual uprightness' won in the end. And why? – because most of the arguments I had advanced to explain away what I did not *wish* to believe had demanded much more credulity than the facts I was endeavouring to repudiate. In other words, I had displayed what I have since come to observe in other fanatical disbelievers, namely the credulity of the sceptic!

This admittedly sounds paradoxical, yet is it so in reality? For, as an example, who is the more credulous, the atheist who believes that the Universe is the outcome of sheer chance, or the religionist who believes that it was formed by a Supreme Intelligence? True, the sceptic can argue like the child: 'If God made the world out of nothing, then who made God'? But to that the philosopher can and has answered: 'There is and never was such a thing as 'Nothing' (another seeming paradox) and as God is Something, there equally never was a time when 'He' did not exist'. As we read in the Vedas: 'I projected this Universe from a fragment of Myself, and I remain'. According to Vedanta philosophy life IS, and when we talk of 'loss of life, or lives' we are talking nonsense; what we should say is 'loss of physical forms'.

The actual chain of circumstances which led to my becoming a Vendantist and finally an occultist, Occultism being a complement of Vendanta philosophy, began, strange to say, with my aversion to Christian Science, to which Miss Evelyn Suart, herself an ardent Christian Scientist, first introduced me. Being as I was at the time a dogmatic and, unfortunately, very intolerant agnostic, I was repelled by this American cult, especially after Miss Suart had somewhat naïvely informed me that by Christian Science means she had dispelled a pea-soup fog from over the London area! On the other hand there was no getting round the fact that Christian Science did cure a lot of human ills, and it was sheer blind prejudice to pretend otherwise. But what repelled me was its religious element and the dogmatic smugness of some of its devotees. As I myself was dogmatic, such being human nature I hated others to be likewise! Yet the question was, how to account for the cures without bringing in the religious element?

Thus Christian Science was among the first non-agnostic cults I tried to explain away, and in that attempt I read a number of books which threw a new light on the subject and on metaphysical healing in general. I remember that among them was a book by Dr. T. J. Hudson entitled *The Law of Psychic Phenomena*, the writer of which explained almost everything by, and ascribed wellnigh miraculous powers to what he called 'The Subconscious Mind'. He stated that he had cured numerous people of rheumatism simply by impressing his subconscious mind to do so before he fell asleep at night. All this I found so satisfactory as a plausible refutation, so I imagined, of Christian Science, and even Spiritualism, another cult I thought was all nonsense, that the subconscious 'mind' theory satisfied me for quite a time as an 'explain-all'. Even so, the gods decreed that the end of my seeking was only to come, and in quite a different way from what I expected, after I had met with a book called Râja Yoga, by Swâmi Vivekânanda. In fine, the study of this to me, convincing book was eventually to alter my whole outlook on life and death.

CHAPTER XXII

Why I Have Written Therapeutical Books

DURING the time I was sharing a house in Liverpool with
Charles Bonnier, I often went to stay with some married
cousins, who by way of adding to their other virtues, contrived
to endure my sartorial and further eccentricities without being
noticeably shocked. Mr. Richardson was a cultured, elderly
business man, who suffered from indifferent health which,
though unfortunate for him, was indirectly to prove fortunate
for myself, since it was through him that I came to take an
interest in Naturopathy, and later on in other unorthodox
systems of healing.

I will not go into details, it is enough to say that my cousins
induced me to try the semi-nature-cure diet which they themselves were trying out; and the almost immediate result was
such a vast improvement in my health and spirits, that I took it
up with enthusiasm – much to the distress of my friends, who
told me I would surely kill myself in the end! Nevertheless, they
have all died except one – a staunch vegetarian – and all at a
younger age than I myself have lived to be.

In the circumstances it was not surprising, since no doctor
had told me to alter my eating habits, that my faith in medical
orthodoxy was very much shaken. Even so I had still to realise
that separativeness was the 'besetting sin' where the healing
arts were concerned, and instead of applying the principle of
unity in diversity there was dissension among them. And there
is still, though the hostility is mostly on the part of the orthodox
towards the unorthodox. Nor is it always definite hostility. I
once knew a London doctor, since deceased, who told me that he
had to give it up because his patients got cured too soon! I met
another doctor, who had discovered a means of curing cancer

without surgery, radium etc. yet when he went to the Ministry of Health to explain his method, he was told that nothing could be done about it. This same doctor submitted a book he had written on his treatment to a medical publisher, and it was declined on the grounds that it would have an adverse effect on the sales of the more orthodox books on the subject. The first cancer patient this doctor treated, over thirty years ago, was still well and fit past eighty. Further to all this; a lady I chanced to meet one day told me that she had cured a large growth on a friend's neck by means of *The Biochemic System of Medicine*. She had also cured herself of bad rheumatism. Having never heard of that system, I at once bought books and studied it; and as it is almost as simple – too simple for medical orthodoxy – as it is effective, I was able to cure some of my ailing friends with it. Further, an Australian doctor once told me his cook had developed an intestinal growth which he did not know how to cure; then a herbalist friend of hers cured it completely with some herbal treatment. After hearing that, I began to investigate Herbalism. Next, my interest was aroused in Osteopathy. An osteopath friend has told me that he frequently has to treat patients who for months, and some even for years had been going to hospitals, suffering from bad backs, necks and heads, or all three, only to be told in the end that nothing more could be done for them. Quite a number of them had been ordered to wear some abominable contraption. My friend usually cures most of them in just a few treatments. Finally, after pooh-poohing Homoeopathy because I knew nothing about it – 'contempt prior to investigation' – I was eventually quite converted to it as a truly scientific method of curing disease. Indeed, many of its cures might almost be called 'miracles'. And yet despite these, I come across sufferers nowadays who might be cured by it yet have never even heard of it.

Now I do not wish to decry orthodox doctors, several of whom have been my good friends. Nevertheless, the fact remains that whilst the orthodox profession has succeeded in vanquishing a number of acute, infectious and contagious diseases, it has

signally failed to cure countless sufferers from chronic afflictions. Moreover, it is arrogantly asserted that they are incurable. Yet in disproof of this hundreds of sufferers from chronic
ailments have subsequently been cured by one or other unorthodox method; that is, of course, provided they had had the
good luck to hear of one. But how many people do? And that is
just the trouble.

It was during the thirties, after I had over many years been
collecting data from every available source, that I wrote my
first therapeutical book and submitted it to a well-know firm of
publishers. The upshot was that their advisory readers told
them not to touch it on any account. However, the chairman of
the company happened to be very friendly with Lord H———,
at the time a highly important personage in the orthodox
medical world: and this worthy peer after reading the script
said: 'Though the book is against us, I should publish it all the
same if I were you'. . . . By a lucky chance Lord H——— was
one of the 'big-wigs' I had favourably quoted in my book!

I wrote that volume – to be followed later by others – at a
time when my name as a musical composer was much more
frequently before the public than it is now. And I was amused
after its publication to see in big letters in one of the illustrated
daily papers, FAMOUS BRITISH COMPOSER FLAYS THE DOCTORS(!)
Just one of these journalistic exaggerations, of course. Actually
my object in writing it had been to try and explode the pernici-
ous lie that all unorthodox methods of healing were nothing
but quackery. . . . And I have been well rewarded. Although it
may be gratifying to receive now and then a complimentary
letter about my music, it is far more gratifying to hear from
sundry unfortunates who, having been doomed to suffer for
years from some painful affliction and been told that they were
incurable, have then cured themselves in a very short time by
this or that simple means or remedy to which I had drawn
attention in one or other of my books.

But now to get back to earlier events.

CHAPTER XXIII

I Establish Myself in London

I N my mid-twenties I left Liverpool and my good friend
Charles Bonnier, partly because it seemed better for my
career to settle in London, and partly because of the kindness
of his character. He thought that domestic duties were getting
too much for his aged nurse, who had been looking after our
little *ménage* and therefore he and she should henceforth live
in furnished apartments; consequently we had to part. Not
long afterwards he retired, and went to live near Cannes,
where at no ripe old age, he eventually died. I like to think
that this selfless and original soul is now enjoying his well-
deserved 'celestial holiday'.

Two unfurnished rooms were found for me, by a girl with
whom I was enjoying a romance, in King's Road, Chelsea, just
opposite where the famous Ellen Terry lived. They were in
the house of an Irish dressmaker, who treated me well, and
was apparently no stickler for the conventions, since she made
no objections to young ladies visiting me without a chaperone;
a thing which in those days was considered highly improper . .
. . Prior to my settling in, an old man was to be seen one
morning driving a cart along the King's Road, and in the cart,
without any covering, was a peculiar assortment of objects
which looked as if they had been abstracted from some chapel.
My father had previously informed me that he had made
arrangements for the transport of my furniture, and that is
what the cart contained. But why it should arrive in such a
vehicle, strange to relate, I never had the curiosity to inquire.

Chelsea was to be my permanent abode for several years,
during which time I made frequent visits to Germany, Paris,
and Switzerland where my friend and benefactor Mr. Hans

Lüthy had retired after giving up his business in Liverpool. At such times as I visited Berlin to see Melchior Lechter and Stefan George (when the poet happened to be there) I stayed with the eminent Egyptologist and his wife, Alan Gardiner, later to become Sir Alan Gardiner, whom I first contacted through his brother Balfour. The A.G.'s were the most entertaining and stimulating hosts, and I cannot write too gratefully of their kindness to me in those days before the first world war and before evil times had descended on 'The Fatherland'. Not only were they hospitable and put up with my eccentricities, but they extended their kindness to my friends (Lechter and others) at whose eccentricities of a somewhat different sort they were indulgently amused. Alan Gardiner being a savant with a scientific intellect and Lechter and myself both having become ardent occultists, many and long were the arguments between us, each of us retaining our own opinions at the end.

In London I had made considerable headway as regards my musical career, had 'moved in Society', and had contrived to collect enough admirers to make the recitals I gave periodically at the Bechstein Hall (now the Wigmore Hall) if not exactly an enriching proposition, at least one on which I lost no money. Good vocalists, both male and female, were generous enough to give their services gratuitously. These recitals consisted entirely of my own works, and I played the piano solos myself and the piano part in chamber music.

It was at one of these functions that with the assistance of a fine violinist, Ethel Barnes, I produced my first Violin Sonata (published by Schott of Mainz), a lengthy and difficult work written for the most part in irregular rhythm – a revolutionary procedure in those days, shocking to the academics. Yet, such was the lack of observation on the part of the critics that, although most of them slanged it, not one of them detected its rhythmic irregularity! Later on at a subsequent recital I produced the *Piano Sonata*, which still later Percy Grainger played in U.S.A., and which his audiences 'swallowed' without distaste, and apparently even with relish.

I had expected that Robin Legge, the then critic of the *Daily Telegraph*, would give it a frightful slating, but to my intense surprise he wrote a most favourable notice; surprise, because he was a severe critic who took himself and his activities very seriously. We were on the most friendly terms, but he was obsessed with the idea that friendship must never interfere with judgment; for which, of course, there is something to be said. All the same it did seem strange to find oneself lunching one day at his hospitable house, only a few days later to see that he had written a number of very unpleasant things about one in his paper. But then, as cynics are wont to remark, 'the sort of criticism you get is largely dependent on what the critic has had for dinner!'

By the time I had reached my late twenties I was already regarded as the musical *enfant terrible* of the Edwardian Age, some music-lovers liking me for my *enfant terriblism* and others scandalized by it and hating me for it.

Among notabilities there were some who started as my foes and ended as friends, one of these being the late Sir Landon Ronald who in middle life became Principal of the Guildhall School of Music. 'I used to loathe your stuff,' he said to me, 'and call you every name under the sun. But I take it all back.' Subsequently he got me to conduct some of my orchestral works at one of his concerts in Birmingham. He himself conducted a few of my works in London. At one time I saw him fairly often, and usually found him in the throes of some romance, for despite his ugliness, of which he used to make fun himself, he seemed to have much success with the ladies . . . I was not over-flush with money in those days – not that I am by any means rich now – and thought that with his influence he might be able to get me some composition pupils. 'But, my dear fellow', he said, 'people think you don't know the rules, so how can I?'

Nevertheless, later on, though not through Landon Ronald, I did have some pupils, one of them being an enthusiastic American whose Americanisms jarred on me so much –

though they ought not to have done – that I was not sorry when he went back to his own country. For when I would play him something to illustrate how things should go in reputable compositions, he would say: 'Gee! that's swell. That's bully,' till in the end the poverty of his vocabulary so got on my nerves that I was at some pains to remain polite. I also had one or two piano pupils, among them a gloomy young man who came to the lessons without having adequately practised, and who would lose his temper when he bungled passages, the effect on me being that I wanted to laugh, and had to push my chair further and further back from the piano so that he could not see my merriment.

Much later in my life, a pianist and teacher who ran a music school of his own asked me to instruct a spate of young ladies in general musicality, if that is the right word; but for some reason, after a couple of terms the number dwindled down to two – and soon to none at all.

But I have been running ahead. Although by my late twenties I had, so to say, 'arrived', by that I do not mean to imply that the important music institutions had ceased to regard me as a 'law-breaker' and a bad influence to be discouraged at all costs. As against that, however, fashionable private singing teachers, male and female, taught my songs to their many pupils, one such teacher being a rotund Austrian, named Victor Beigel, who at least had the honour of instructing our delightful radio-artist Freddy Grisewood. I say, 'at least', because Beigel was not an altogether admirable character, having acquired all his knowledge from the really great *lieder*-singer, Von Zur Mühlen, for whom he had acted as accompanist during the lessons. Von Zur Mühlen had settled in London, and the stipulation was that Beigel (who could hardly sing himself) should not set up as a teacher in the same town. Thus, the fat, bald-headed Austrian had broken his contract, and 'done the dirty' on the very man to whom he should have been grateful.

Around the time of which I write, there were still some

people who, because my music was un-English, would refer to me as 'The English Debussy'. Yet although Professor Norman Demuth, for one, points out that the sobriquet was entirely unjustified,* it is only fair to say that in my earliest days I did owe somethng to the eminent Frenchman, but not more so than to Richard Strauss. Indeed, two orchestral Rhapsodies I wrote in my early twenties were so Straussian that I subsequently consigned them both to limbo. Comparisons of course are odious, but every composer is influenced at first by some other composer. Beethoven was influenced by Haydn, and Strauss himself by Wagner. The Straussian phase, however, was only a passing one with me. On the other hand, my *Aubade* for orchestra (published by Schott) and written somewhat later, has a certain Debussyesque flavour about it, though when I played the work to Debussy himself he would only grant that just one passage was perhaps '*un peu*' like his own music.

But of Debussy I shall write in my next chapter.

* *Musical Trends in the 20th Century* (Rockcliff.)

CHAPTER XXIV

My Recollections of Debussy and Ravel

AROUND the beginning of the century I had made the acquaintance of a composeress (if I may employ the word to match authoress) named Adela Madison, a married woman who moved in London society. And by the way, being of a waggish turn of mind, I could not resist the temptation to concoct an absurd conundrum round her name, which ran;

If Adela Madison is the daughter of her father's daddy's son,
Then what relation is Adela Madison
To the sister of her father's daddy's son?

Not seeing it written, my friends used to puzzle over this fatuous doggerel for quite a time . . . However, to ascend from the ridiculous to the more serious, Mrs. Madison, now many years deceased, used to write recherché songs in the French style, having, so she hinted, had a romance with the eminent composer Gabriel Fauré, and possibly some lessons from him too; though whether the lessons came about as the result of the romance of vice versa, I was not told. In any case, Mrs. Madison had everything good to say about French music and everything bad to say about the very academic British type which prevailed at the time. It was, in fact, because I had not followed this academic trend but had gone my own wilful way and scandalized the professors, that Mrs. Madison took an interest in me. 'You must come to Paris', she had said, 'and I will somehow arrange for you to meet Gabriel Fauré, Debussy and Ravel.'

It was not long before she fulfilled her promise. She knew Mme. Bardac, who soon afterwards became Debussy's second wife; and so, as the first step, I was taken to see that rather plump and affable *femme du monde*, whose face, I remember, was powdered to an exceeding pallor and whose amber-coloured hair was obviously dyed; all of which struck me in those days when respectable English women did not make up, as typically and amusingly French! But what amused me still more was the fact that, whilst Mme. Bardac told us that she would be enchanted to let me meet Debussy, she hoped we wouldn't mind if she invited him one *afternoon* instead of an evening, as he always liked to come in an enormous wide-awake – and she made a sweeping gesture with her arm as if his hat were going to fill the whole room! Why all this business about hats should have exercised her mind – considering that polite males do not usually wear their hats in the house – was due to an absurd custom which obliged gentlemen to bring these headgear, silk ones at that, into the drawing-room when greeting their hostess. Thus, a few days later, my first impression of Debussy was that of a sallow, crinkly-haired, black-bearded and rather quiet man, uncomfortably nursing a large cowboy-like hat, the while he rolled cigarettes with an astonishing and enviable dexterity.

Frenchmen have said that he would have passed unnoticed in the street; but for me he had both an unusual and kindly face . . . I think he was somewhat ill at ease that afternoon at Mme. Bardac's. Being asked to meet and size up a young composer from England, with its bad musical reputation, was a matter likely to arouse all his scepticism and to bore and embarrass him as well. For, as I learnt when I got to know him better, he was no adept at polite prevarication where music was concerned. If he liked a thing he said so, but if confronted with something academic or commonplace, he curtly dismissed it as ugly, banal or vulgar. At the time of which I write, Charpentier's opera *Louise* was having considerable success in Paris, and when I happened to mention that I had been to hear it, he said: 'How can you go to listen to such vulgar stuff?' As for other contemporary composers, hardly any of whom he liked, the venom of his criticisms was only lessened because of the

Firmly Yrs
Percy Grainger
Nov. 1915.

. Percy Aldridge Grainger, Australian composer. A lifelong friend and fellow
tudent. He and I, together with Roger Quilter, Balfour Gardiner and Norman
O'Neill, later became known in England as 'The Frankfurt Group'.

6*a*. Iwan Knorr, my broadminded Professor of Harmony, Counterpoint and Composition at the Hochs'che Conservatorium, Frankfurt am Main.

6*b*. Lionel Tertis and myself rehearsing my Viola work together.

dispassionate manner in which they were uttered. His attitude towards some of the classical masters was equally uncompromising, especially towards Beethoven, to whom he uncharitably and irreverently referred as *le vieux sourd*.

But I am now speaking of the days when Debussy had already married Mme. Bardac, and after he had given me a standing invitation to dine with him and his wife every time I came to Paris, the object of this kindness to a young composer seventeen years his junior being that I should play him my latest 'indiscretions'. These auditions, so to say, took place in what had become Debussy's study, and I was astonished at its extreme tidiness. There was nothing the least bohemian about this elegantly furnished room. Not a thing was out of its place, not a manuscript to be seen anywhere. The latest score on which the composer was at work was hidden in a large, embossed portfolio which reposed tidily on his desk. On the shelves, much to my surprise, for he spoke no English, was a whole row of books by Rudyard Kipling, which I glanced at while he had gone to bid an elaborate goodnight to his little daughter, of whom he was intensely fond. Whether all the orderliness was due to his wife's influence, or whether he was one of those 'rare birds', a tidy genius, was a delicate matter I could not well inquire into, though now I am sorry I did not. Such neatness was in fact quite in keeping with Debussy's music, which is essentially refined, neat and delicate at times, yet never weak in invention. These characteristics, I suggest, give the clue to his dislike of Beethoven, and also to much that he disliked in his eminent German contemporary, Richard Strauss.

'The ingenuity of his orchestration', Debussy remarked to me, 'excites my admiration. But as for the rest, he is most banal.'

But then this exclusive Frenchman had no liking for Germany or anything German. When one evening I mentioned my student days in Frankfurt, with a gesture of disdain, he called Germany 'the land of stoves and professors' (it alliterates in French) and proceeded to congratulate me on having escaped

E

its influence. Even so, his fulminations against the Teutonic composers were not quite consistent, for on another occasion he confessed to a fondness for Schumann.

Before my visits to this famous Frenchman came to an end, he generously did me a service by writing a laudatory paragraph about me for publication, though I myself had not asked him to do so, the request having come from Messrs. B. Schotts Sons, of Mainz.

On one of my periodical visits to Germany I had made a contact with this celebrated firm (Wagner's original publishers) and its owner, Dr. Ludwig Strecker, senior, who, having become interested in some of my smaller works through my English publisher Mr. Elkin, had resolved to publish several of my larger ones. Despite England's poor reputation where music was concerned, Dr. Strecker had come to have faith in me. Nevertheless, as a matter of good policy, he decided to obtain some opinions about me from a few musicians of eminence so that they could be printed in the 'Cyril Scott Catalogue', Debussy being one of the musicians to whom he applied. And not only did the French tone-poet willingly comply, but wrote something so generous that it revealed the innate quality of his character, and incidentally served to dispel the notion that his biting criticisms of so many of his fellow composers were inspired by professional jealousy or egotism. Indeed, as regards the latter, hardly ever did he speak of his own music, at any rate to me. Only on one occasion did he touch on the subject, and then it was to make a melancholy admission. 'I have come to the end of my tether,' he said, in effect. 'My music has its limitations. Yours permits of further expansion, mine does not. You will go ahead; I have written myself out.' That was, I think, in 1913, the last time I was ever to see him. Five years later he died.

What a very different personality was Maurice Ravel! He was one of those rapidly-talking Frenchmen with a rather schoolboy-like type of wit which most of his associates found highly entertaining. In stature he was so small and slender that if he had not been a composer he might have made an excellent jockey!

When I first met him, he presented a most extraordinary appearance. His face was adorned with a moustache and short side-whiskers, closely cropped, but no beard, though later on that was added for a time. As for his clothes, he was dressed in a tail coat, not the usual black sort, but one with a very loud pattern, with trousers to match. He reminded me of those carciatures which used to appear in *Punch* about a hundred years ago. Mrs. Madison, who effected the introduction, regarded him as a freak, and musically as a rather intriguing experimentalist. He had been a pupil of her friend Gabriel Fauré (whom I met once only) and who thought highly of his gifts, though he did not always immediately approve of his too daring deviations from the classical tradition. I say 'immediately', because when he got used to them he altered his opinion. It speaks well for Ravel that he loved and revered his teacher, and never forgot the debt of gratititude he owed to that muscian of rare quality and insight.

Ravel was never the least stand-offish or reluctant to discuss his compositions with fellow-composers whom he happened to like. Although I was four years his junior, he was always ready to play to me his latest works, and as he expected me to 'return the compliment', we became for a time a sort of 'mutual encouragement society'. He was not even above asking my advice, and after playing some daring passage would ask: 'Do you think I have gone too far? Ought I to tone it down a bit?'

Being a remarkably dexterous pianist, he could give an excellent impression of either chamber-music or orchestral works on the piano. Sometimes he would attempt to sing as well, and then the effect was unintentionally comic, for he had what my professor, Iwan Knorr, used to call a 'regular composer's voice'!

Often we used to meet in the *salon* of a musical 'lion hunter' named Mme. de St. Marceau. She was evidently no stickler for etiquette, for though her parties were in the evening, Ravel used to arrive in his astonishing get-up and play to the company, which included the distinguished composer Florent Schmitt.

Like Debussy, Ravel had an aversion in general to German music and its influence. Also, like Debussy, he had an intense fondness for cats! But in other respects the two composers were widely dissimilar in temperament. Debussy, in his younger days, is said to have had numerous love-affairs, Ravel apparently had none, a most unusual thing in a composer, considering that musicians are notoriously amorous and romantic. And yet if he was not a lover of the fair sex, neither was he a woman hater, a fact evidenced from his long friendship with Mme. Jordan-Morhange. True, romance-seekers have suggested that he really loved this widow, but was too shy and diffident to ask her hand in marriage. Yet why seek to make him out to have been a less unusual character than was actually the case? Just as religious mystics have found women unnecessary for their happiness, so may Ravel, seeing that he was a Nature-mystic, as nearly all his music reveals.

After the first world war I only saw him on those rare occasions when he visited England. By that time he had got rid of his unbecoming facial decorations, but he still retained his slender, jockey-like figure and all his other characteristics. Success had not spoilt him in any way; he was as sociable and un-stand-offish as he had ever been, and still in some respects as schoolboy-like.

Although I myself had long since acquired an aversion to playing my latest compositions to friends, not so apparently Ravel, for the last time I saw him at the house of some mutual acquaintances he played to us his latest Violin Sonata (minus a violinist) and made comments to me while he played the work. I have forgotten what the comments were, but even without them it would have been obvious to me that his style had materially changed. His work had become thinner in texture, so it seemed to me, and more discordant. I did not get the chance to ask him if some of his tastes had also changed or to tell him that some of my own had undergone a transformation since the days when we first fraternised in Paris. In those days our opinions differed mostly about Tchaikovsky, whose music still appealed to me, whereas Ravel had dismissed him as the 'most vulgar and meretricious of all the Russians', and had wondered how I could possibly admire him. Yet although Ravel's verdict was over-severe, I must confess that my erstwhile enthusiasm for the popular Russian has long since somewhat waned, and that the melodic vulgarities which jarred on my friend have for me, albeit with some exceptions, become more marked with the passage of time. . . . And so Ravel has won in the end, and I only wish he were still here for me to tell him so.

CHAPTER XXV

I Join the Theosophical Movement

IT is curious that my interest in Theosophy and the Higher Occultism should first have been awakened through a Christian Scientist, a young American singer who was living in London. He was a strange though agreeable fellow who suffered from an 'indecision complex' about his name. First he called himself one thing and then another, and for all I know he may have altered his name a third time when he returned to America, where he died only a few years after we had met.

During the time of our short acquaintanceship, Mrs. (later Dr.) Annie Besant, of Theosophical fame, came to London from India to lecture, and my singer friend, despite being a Christian Scientist persuaded me to go with him to hear her. Mrs. Besant was then at the height of her powers, and after hearing her first few sentences I at once realised that she was a very great orator, the more so, seeing her oratory was devoid of all bombast and emotionalism. But what struck me in addition was the unassailable logic of all her utterances. Here was something, I thought, worthy of looking into and studying; it was not incompatible with Yoga Philosophy, and perhaps might even be its complement. And this surmise, I was later on to discover, was true.

Meanwhile, I read all the books on Theosophy I could get and devoured them in my spare time. Indeed, the more I studied the literature, the more did I find that it supplied the details of which Indian Philosophy was only the outline. The fact that the Theosophical Movement had been started by Mme. Blavatsky, an alleged impostor, carried no weight with me, considering that most persons who upset conventional, religious or other notions, invariably collect detractors.

Besides which, how was her prodigious literary output to be accounted for: *Isis Unveiled*, two large volumes, and *The Secret Doctrine*, three large volumes? People who merely wanted to impose on the public would neither be capable of such a Herculean task nor would they have wished to go to the trouble of writing millions of words when a few conjuring tricks might have served their nefarious purpose.

In short, the slanderous legend about Mme. Blavatsky was but another example of the credulity of the sceptic! She had also been accused of inventing the Mahatmas, Adepts, High Initiates, Masters of Wisdom, by whatever name one elects to call them, even though other persons had likewise contacted them and hence could vouch for their existence. . . And who had been primarily responsible for all this slander? – the Christian missionaries in Madras! And so, as *I* was not a member of the legion of 'credulous sceptics', I accepted the existence of The Hierarchy of Initiates, or Great White Lodge as it is called; though I should certainly have been very surprised to hear that not so long hence I would contact one of those Initiates myself, or better said, that any of them would wish to contact *me*. But I shall deal with that anon.

Through studying Theosophy I came to learn that there are Supermen, or the highest type of sages, who by reason of their much longer evolution, have developed certain powers and perceptive faculties which *as yet* are merely latent in the generality of mankind, but will eventually come into manifestation. Thus the difference between a High Initiate and an ordinary man is only one of *degree* but not of kind. Although these Supermen have reached Liberation, a certain number of them none the less retain their physical bodies as points of focus, so to say, that thereby they may the more be able to serve humanity. Yet they are not limited to their physical bodies, for they can centre their consciousness at any point of the world, or, if necessary, materialise a body wherever they may desire. Alternatively, they can appear in one of their subtler *bodies* to such disciples who possess sufficient clairvoyance to perceive them. (Spiritualists might call them 'High Guides'). When I first read of all this, I had of course to take it merely on trust, but since those days, I have come to know through the actual evidence that what I read was true.

A part of The Masters' very extensive work consists of endeavours telepathically to impress on receptive minds ideas and ideals for the betterment of man, be they connected with philosophy, religions, science, art, literature, music or ideologies. I have advisedly said 'endeavours', because even the Masters may not interfere with the measure of free-will with which the human race has been endowed. They can only seek to guide, but never to *force* mankind to tread the paths of wisdom instead of folly; and in consequence, many of the cults and trends of thought which they inspire, become corrupted and perverted, often to serve evil and selfish ends. Moreover, human nature being what it is, a large percentage of people are the worst advertisements for the particular cause they themselves espouse.

When I first joined the Theosophical Society – years ago – I was naïve enough to imagine, from theosophical literature, that all its members would be persons of unusually fine calibre who lived up to the theosophical principle of Brotherhood to the fullest degree. But I was soon to find myself greatly disillusioned; though I am far from implying that there were not a number of very charming, noble and selfless souls among its members, and still are. Yet, as against these, I encountered adherents who were largely preoccupied with their own imagined importance, and were as narrow-minded, intolerant and straight-laced within the confines of the new cult they had embraced as is any ultra-orthodox Christian sectarian.

The Theosophical *Movement* itself had been inspired by two Indian High Initiates known as the Masters K. H. (Koot Hoomi) and M. (Morya) who for that purpose had used the ever-devoted, self-sacrificing and greatly gifted, if eccentric, Mme Blavatsky as their instrument, medium and willing servant. But the Theosophical Movement *is*, and always *was* intended to be a much larger and all-embracing cult than the Theosophical

Society, just as was the Christian religion, as opposed to any one of its numerous narrow sects. Nevertheless, the quite untheosophical dogma arose that the Masters could only be contacted by members of the Theosophical Society, and only by special members who were counted worthy to join the so-termed Esoteric Section at that. In short, that unpleasant reptile, 'spiritual' snobbery, was found creeping among the community. Furthermore, there were scandals from time to time; but that is a detail, for scandals are apt to occur in any Society. Much more regrettable was the labelling of certain members as Initiates, when their behaviour was not of a kind to warrant such an assumption. One woman member, if my recollection is not at fault, was even alleged to have been the Virgin Mary! – though I am not implying that *her* conduct was unexemplary. But I do say that when it comes to revelations about spiritual status and past lives, most of them are quite unreliable unless made by a Master. And in any case one does not publicize them.

One of the things which puzzled me when I first became acquainted with Occultism was how the Masters, living respectively in various parts of the world, should be able to contact likely media for their work. The answer is, roughly and briefly stated, that in the auras of men of good-will who sincerely wish to help their fellows, there is a certain revealing luminosity which attracts the attention of the Initiates, as does a light in the surrounding darkness. There are, admittedly, other factors in many cases involved, but lengthy explanations are outside the scope of these *Confessions*.

Which reminds me that I still have to confess that via Occultism I came to see the Christian religion from, to me, an entirely new angle; for I learned that there is an occult or esoteric side to that Faith, and one which struck me as an entirely logical exegesis.

E*

CHAPTER XXVI

The Years Before the First World War

AFTER living for a few years in Chelsea, I shared an upper apartment with a friend in Queen's Road, Bayswater, near William Whiteleys. But as in those days Queen's Road was infested with barrel-organs and the like, there soon came a time when I could stand the nuisance no longer, and so decided to share a little house in a quieter street with another friend.

It was in this little house that I later on gave lessons to the one pupil who was eventually to make a distinguished name for himself in the musical world, namely Edmund Rubbra. But I doubt whether I was much use to him, for I think it far better for students to study at Institutions where they can mingle with other students and hear their works performed. Realising this, Rubbra had the *nous* to leave me and go to the R.C.M. – since when he has become famous, whilst his erstwhile teacher has receded into the background. Not that this is without advantages; for I still maintain what I wrote some years ago in one of my books, that 'fame wastes a young man's time and tires an old man's body'.

At the time of which I write, Continental pianists and violinists when visiting London would pay me the compliment of calling on me so as to get my own interpretation of my works. I was then in my thirties. One day, to my surprise and gratification, I received a letter from abroad which turned out to be from the widow of Gustav Mahler. She apologised for being so unconventional as to write to me without an introduction, but said that she couldn't resist the urge to do so because she admired my works and had spent many interesting hours playing my *Violin Sonata* (No. 1) with her brother-in-law,

Prof. Rosé of the Rosé Quartet. Prof. Rosé had originally come across my 'Americanesque' *Tallahassee Suite*, which so took his fancy that he wrote to Schotts' for more of my works. When later on I met the charming and beautiful Frau Mahler in Vienna, she amused me by telling me that the Professor had somehow got it into his head that I was an old gentleman of eighty! – an idea which, however, was dispelled when he received my *Violin Sonata*.

My contact with Frau Mahler indirectly led to performances of one or more of my orchestral works in the Austrian capital, and to meetings with several notable musicians, one of them being Eugen D'Albert, who proceeded to arrange an evening of my chamber works, coupled with those of Delius, at the *Tonkünstler Verein*, of which he was the President. Although now more or less forgotten, he was among the most renowned pianists of his time, had written a successful Opera called *Tiefland* and, incidentally, before he died had had no less than six wives. I saw him several times in various places during the ensuing years, and as he was a stocky little man with a bald head and a high piping voice, though otherwise very agreeable, I could not help wondering why he should be so attractive to women – at least before they really got to know him through the propinquity afforded by marriage. However that may be, it seems that he so exasperated his respective wives that (as he told my publisher, Herr Strecker) one of them used to tear up his manuscripts and another to attack him with the curtain pole. To say the least, he was certainly a very unconventional Englishman, for despite his name, he was English born, his father having been a dancing master who – curious coincidence – had given my 'duchessy' Aunt Louise dancing lessons.

How much his generous attitude towards my works added to my prestige is difficult to say. In any case the Vienna *Tonkünstler Verein* was not the only organisation of the kind which paid me the compliment of giving 'Cyril Scott Evenings', for the *Tonkünstler Vereins* both in Frankfurt and in Cologne gave whole programmes devoted to my works, followed by suppers in my honour at the end. On these occasions I played my *Piano Sonata* (No. 1.) and cursed myself for having made it so difficult, especially as, in Cologne, my erstwhile teacher, Herr Uzielli, was present and I wished to do him credit. I also played some minor pieces on that occasion, including the *Waterwagtail*, and I remember that he reproached me afterwards for just 'rattling it off' as if I were bored with it – which in fact I *was*.

If I remember rightly, my first visit to Vienna was around 1913, and I did not return to that delightful city, as it then was, till 1922, the war of /14–18 having intervened. On my second visit I played my *Piano Concerto*, which was very favourably received, and which in the interim I had already played in London, and in several towns in America where I had toured in /20–21. But of that later.

I recall that during my second stay in Vienna, that amazing pianist Walter Gieseking gave a recital there and included my *Deuxieme Suite*, which like the *Piano Sonata* ends with a very difficult fugue. Incidentally, when I used to play this to Herr Uzielli's first wife, she said it was so exciting that it gave her palpitations! and even the very critical Delius called it 'fine, strong stuff'. I merely mention this, however, because many of my critics were wont to dismiss me as 'precious', and incapable of writing anything forceful. When Gieseking played it on the occasion concerned, he did not know that I was in Vienna, and was very surprised to see me after the recital in the artists' room.

I have referred to him as 'amazing', because apart from his other qualities, his capacity to read at sight was simply dumbfounding. When years later I placed the manuscript of my *2nd Piano Sonata* before him, (a formidable work to play) he read it straight off, making hardly a mistake.

In Vienna a performance was given of a work I then called *An Overture to Princesse Maleine* (a Maeterlinck play), but although I received an enthusiastic letter about it from Frau Mahler, I was not sufficiently satisfied with the composition as it stood, and many years later I re-worked it and called it *A Festival Overture*, in which guise it won the *Daily Telegraph* prize.

To digress for a moment; I am one of those people who do not hold with the policy of raking up and performing early and unrepresentative works of composers, works written perhaps long before they had developed their respective styles. Such a policy is neither fair to the deceased or maybe still living composers, and is boring for the public. How often have I been bored 'to the fidgets' by having at some concert been obliged to listen to some long and early work by A. or B. or C. merely because it was by one or the other. Hence I resolved that, however unlikely it might be, I would never risk placing the public in that unpleasant position in regard to my own works. Consequently, unless they were published and it was already too late, I destroyed practically all my orchestral scores written prior to my *Two Passacaglias* (on Irish Airs) composed *circa* 1912. There may be such a thing as 'better late than never', but to my mind there is equally such a thing, where music is concerned, as 'better never than late'.

The *Two Passacaglias* were first produced at The Royal Philharmonic Society, and later on performed elsewhere. But though they were well received, their stars were evidently not propitious ones, for when my late publisher, Mr. William Elkin, after a decent lapse of time wrote to the Committee suggesting that in view of their success another work by me might perhaps be contemplated, the reply was that the Society 'considered it had already done its duty by Cyril Scott' – and there the matter ended. Since when the R.P.S., as far as I know, has never produced another of my works, its duty towards me having, it would seem, been liquidated once and for all.

The stars under which I composed the *Piano Concerto*, written at the same period, seem to have been equally unpropitious. For Sir Thomas Beecham, after producing it with myself as the soloist at the Queen's Hall, was in process of fixing up an extensive tour with me and it on the Continent – when the first world war came and frustrated the whole scheme.

I am not in a position to know how many Continental or American pianists have since taken up that work, but think I am right in saying that the only two British artists who have played it are Miss Esther Fisher, in a B.B.C. studio concert during the thirties, and Mr. Kendall Taylor, also at a studio concert on my seventieth birthday. Both artists gave very fine performances. As for myself, since its inception I have been engaged to play it twice at very long intervals at 'The Proms' and once, I think, at Bournemouth under the baton of Sir Dan Godfrey. There was also to have been a performance of it at the Hallé Concerts in Manchester with Albert Coates as the conductor, but when it came to the final rehearsal, he threw down his baton and said; 'We can't possibly do this work with such few rehearsals. I dare not risk it': and so I had to play piano solos instead. Incidentally, I have heard in a roundabout way that when some pianists have been asked why they do not take up the 'Scott Concerto', which would give them a chance to show off their brilliant technique, the answer has been, 'He plays it himself', implying that they have not wished to encroach on my preserves! That of course may have been merely an excuse, but in any case it is very difficult for artists to play works that are out of the usual rut, for as soon as they propose such items, the concert-promoters insist that they should play some hackneyed concerto; a fact I know from what certain eminent pianists have told me themselves after their having suggested my own work.

As for my personal opinion of the *Piano Concerto* from the compositional standpoint, I would say it is simply what I intended it to be, not a deep work but just an enlivening one. I used to say facetiously of the 1st movement, 'It is as if Scarlatti had lived in China'! Admittedly there are some parts in that movement I would like to change, for I made a too frequent use of a chord which I have since deleted from my harmonic 'vocabulary'. Even so, my late friend, Frederic Austin, took the trouble to write me after the performance in /49 that the work 'sounded as fresh as ever'! – I also received some other complimentary letters about it. . . With regard to the last movement I unashamedly used a sort of neo-Handelian idiom, not because

I had any leanings towards neo-classicism as a trend, but simply because 'it came like that' for that particular work. Since the *Concerto* makes no great demands on the intellect, since it has always aroused generous applause when performed – I am now including performances in America – it is conceivable that had the British public been given the chance really to get to know it at an earlier date, it might have gained the kind of popularity which, say, the Max Bruch *Violin Concerto* achieved. But perhaps 'I say it as shouldn't'.

CHAPTER XXVII

1914 – and after

BEING endowed with imagination, which has both advantages and drawbacks, I have never been physically courageous, though it would seem that I do not lack moral courage. I remember after one of my lectures in America (1921) that a lady came to me and exclaimed admiringly; 'I don't know how you have the courage to get up and say such things'. Yet I was not even aware that *that* virtue came into the matter at all.

Nevertheless I have since come to the obvious conclusion that moral courage arises from the absence of a particular sort of vanity, whereas physical courage is more than often associated with a lack of imagination plus the possession of 'good, strong nerves'! – and evidently the two things are seldom combined. I have never forgotten the remark made to me during the First War by an acquaintance who had been rejected because of his eyes or something. He said: 'If only to God they would take me. I feel such an ass walking about in 'civvies' when everyone else is in khaki!'

My activities between 1914 and /18 were somewhat varied. Being exempt from military service and hence possessing my freedom, it struck me that the best thing to do was to make myself useful by playing at concerts in connection with War Charities, of which there were a large number. This playing for charity purposes was to stand me in good stead, for towards the end of the war I was hauled up for medical re-examination, put into the C3 category, and finally served with a notice obliging me to do clerical work. But as it fortunately happened, during the summer of 1918, I played at a concert at Harlech, North Wales, at which Lloyd George, then Prime Minister, was present. A few days later I received a telegram from him inviting me to tea at his house in Criccieth, in company with my host and friend A. L. Coburn (distinguished American photographer) who had wanted to take his photograph. The upshot was that when Lloyd George learned that I had been called up to do a clerical job, he said it was absurd, and that a special committee ought to have been formed to deal with cases like mine. And so, through his kindly intervention, I remained a free man. . . But as I have said, that was when the war was nearing its end.

Meanwhile I had made a journey to Florence as the guest of two old friends who had taken a villa there for the autumn and winter of 1914–15. In that wonderful city I was greatly surprised to find myself hailed as a celebrity, and the Leonardo da Vinci Society arranged a whole programme of my works, presenting me after the concert with the Society's medal. In Milan I also found myself regarded as a celebrity, at any rate among the younger musicians and the intelligentsia. It was gratifying to me that my fame (!) had not been acquired through my trifles but through some of my more serious works, mostly those published by Schott of Mainz.

On my way home I decided to break my journey for a few weeks in Switzerland, though I regret to say, not with my erstwhile friends the Lüthys, formerly of Liverpool, seeing that our association had come to an untimely end. For this I can only blame myself and that very disturbing emotion called love. . . The truth is that Mr. Lüthy possessed two attractive daughters, but, as in the Liverpool days they were almost children, they did not then come into the picture. Meanwhile they had grown up, and one of them was so meltingly beautiful that I fell badly in love with her while the guest of my friend at his villa near Vevey. This created a very awkward situation, for although he may have admired me as a musician, the opinions I had come to hold on sex and matrimony were not at all to his liking, and in consequence not only did he object to his daughter having me as her 'boy-friend', but also to the idea of her possibly having me as a husband. To make matters worse, lover-like, we had met in a clandestine manner in Basel, where she was for a time an art student. Discovering this, Mr. Lüthy wrote and called me a scoundrel, which perhaps I was according to the conventional ideas of that time, especially as I had previously flirted with his other daughter, so that the whole thing was what is vulgarly called a thorough mess-up, and through my 'scandalous behaviour' I lost my good friends. As for the romance itself, being largely 'beauty-deep', it ended as most romances of the sort are apt to end.

But all this had happened some years before my 1915 visit to Switzerland, and I mention it as one of those episodes in my disfavour which I the more regretted because I owed so much to the Lüthys for their many kindnesses to me, and had no desire to repay them with what seemed like sheer ingratitude. Besides, having once introduced certain characters to the reader – characters who at one time played rather important parts in my story – I do not wish to leave him wondering what may have become of them. Indeed, the particular visit to Switzerland – this time to Geneva – about which I would write, was for the purpose of seeing again some other 'characters' previously mentioned in this book.

In the chapter dealing with my student days in Frankfurt, I alluded to Professor Hugo Heermann, who had been obliged to leave the Conservatoire because he had committed the indiscretion of kissing one or more of his lady-pupils. Thereafter he had moved to Berlin, where during my visits to that capital I had often been in his company and that of his warm-hearted family, which included two grown-up daughters. Incidentally, with one of these I had had a sentimental friendship – minus kisses – and when I arrived in Geneva, where the family had moved, I found myself acting the role of comforter to the young lady, she having lost her heart to her unreciprocal singing teacher. The Professor (by then an old man), and his wife were as engaging as ever. We talked in the most frank and friendly manner about the war, and I was interested to hear that, as far as my friends knew, the 'Hymn of Hate', about which there was

so much talk in England, was a pure myth, which had obviously
been invented for the sole purpose of stimulating evil emotions.
I also heard that, in the German papers, there was a lot of
verbiage about 'British atrocities', just as in the English papers
there was the same thing about 'German atrocities', but how
much truth was contained in the statements I could never know.

After taking an affectionate farewell of the Heermann parents
in Geneva, I never saw them again. They went to live in Merano,
where they eventually died. But the two daughters I was to see
once more, in Berlin in 1930, and that was for the last time. I
only hope that they were not among the thousands of innocent
victims who perished during the second great holocaust.

CHAPTER XXVIII

Bernard Shaw, George Moore, H. G. Wells and Other Celebrities

D URING the remaining years of the (first) war I was, despite the disturbed mental atmosphere, fairly creative both musically and otherwise. I wrote among other works *La Belle Dame Sans Merci*, for Baritone, Chorus and Orchestra. I also wrote the libretto and finally the music of my first Opera, *The Alchemist*. This latter work was produced in Germany in 1928, and *La Belle Dame Sans Merci* not till during the late thirties, when Sir Thomas Beecham conducted it at one of the Leeds Festivals. As for books, I wrote four in all, one of which was destined to acquire so wide and lengthy a reputation that it sells even now, nearly forty years after it was written. I called it *The Initiate* by *His Pupil*, and it was not until some two decades later that its anonymity was pierced.

Another book I wrote around the same period I entitled *The Adept of Galilee*. Whether this book would have sold as well as *The Initiate* is difficult to say, for soon after its publication a very large percentage of the edition was bombed, and it was never reprinted. Prior to the writing of those two books, the little volume relative to music had appeared under the pretentious title *The Philosophy of Modernism*, which incidentally gave rise to the supposition that it had to do with religion! and it served me right for using such a grandiloquent name. Referring to this book in his *Musical Trends in The 20th Century*, Professor Norman Demuth observes: '. . . he came into the open in the broadest possible manner, and shocked a good many susceptibilities by his outspoken denunciation of ideas hitherto taken for granted.' Since when some of my erstwhile statements shock my own susceptibilities, whilst others have become so widely accepted that nowadays they would not be worth saying.

I began the book with the sententious axiom: 'The prerequisite to immortality in the world of art is the capacity to create something new, or, in other words, the capacity to invent a style'. To which I might have added (but didn't) that whereas it is fairly easy to create a new form of ugliness, it takes a genius to create a new form of *beauty*. What I would retract, however, are some of the rather patronising remarks about Brahms, and more especially my assertions regarding the 'inexpressibility' of music in general. Had I then known about the occult aspects of the tonal art, I would not have quoted and tried to substantiate the fallacious dictum that 'Music expresses nothing but itself'.

It was during those war years that I spent an unforgettable fortnight with Bernard Shaw and his wife, as their guests, at an hotel near Torquay. I had met G.B.S. several times and had lunched with him and Mrs. Shaw when they were still living at Adelphi Terrace. He had a habit of sending a messenger with a note to my little house in Bayswater, saying in effect, 'Do come to lunch to-day at 1 o'clock'. Sometimes he had other guests and sometimes we were quite alone.

Although it is running ahead of my story, the last time I lunched with the great man was when he was eighty-four, and I was struck by the absence of any senility and by the benignity of his expression. In private life G.B.S. was quite different from what many people would imagine from reading his works. He told me, in so many words, that all his apparent conceit and fun-poking at things was a literary ruse to get his message across; in short, the only way to get serious truths over was to say them in an unserious manner.

During that luncheon he imparted to me something relative to Elgar and myself which greatly surprised me. I had only met Elgar once for a few moments and never knew that he took the slightest interest in my works. And yet, when Shaw had on one occasion said to him: 'Why, Elgar, for a British composer you have become quite daring in your harmonies of late', he had answered: 'Yes, but don't forget it was Scott who started it all'. It was a generous though curious remark, and I can only assume he meant that I was the first English composer to side-step the British academicism of the time. Even so, this was not quite correct, for when I first appeared in the arena, Josef Holbrooke was also writing unacademic music and to no small extent dumbfounding the professorial burgher.

As for Shaw's own opinion of myself, he once, in my presence, remarked to a friend: 'Scott is the only British composer in whom I can detect a real style', an admission which I found almost as surprising as that of Elgar. (Mrs. Shaw, by the way, told me that in the evenings G.B.S. as she called him, would often sit down at his piano, play my pieces and even try to sing some of my songs!) This opinion of my style he had already expressed while we were together in Torquay, but he had varied it slightly, for he had told me that I was the only composer of *the younger generation* in whom a style was detectable. But then in those days there was no B.B.C. for him to familiarise himself with the works of Stravinski, Scriabin and others who were of my own generation; and as for playing them himself, they were somewhat beyond his capabilities.

During that visit to Torquay I discovered what contrasting personalities were Shaw and his wife. Whilst he *was*, or pretended to be, an agnostic, she confessed to be something of a mystic, and told me that every morning before breakfast she would engage in mystical meditation for three-quarters of an hour. I was also to discover that her attitude towards sex was one of intolerance and perhaps even of disgust, and from certain things she said I gathered that she had never been what is called a real wife to G.B.S. That he should have married a woman with such Victorian views seemed to me a mystery; and yet apparently they were a harmonious couple. All the same, she was one of his severest critics, and told me in his presence that several of his plays ought to be burnt, at which remark, good-naturedly he merely laughed. . . Which reminds me that he confessed to finding the production of any of his plays more or less a torture, for hardly ever did the actors and actresses say his lines in the way he liked. The trouble was they always wanted to *act* instead of letting the plays act themselves. 'You can be thankful you're a musician and not a playwright', he said.

I saw G.B.S. for the last time in 1938, and then came the second world war and I was all the time in Somerset and Devon. When it ended he was a very old man, and although I might have gone to see him at his house in the country, I thought it kinder to keep away, and wrote him to that effect. When he died, despite my belief in personal survival, I was deeply moved and had a very painful lump in my throat, for not only had I lost a friend but the whole world had lost a most lovable character and a unique wit.

Between 1914 and some years later I was fairly often in the company of other notable men of letters, one of them being George Moore. I used to meet him over week-ends at the country mansion of the very wealthy sister of Dame Ethel Smyth. Her name was Mrs. Charles Hunter, and as she was fond of entertaining celebrities, malicious persons called her 'Mrs. Lion-Hunter'. One of her great friends was John Sargent, the painter, several of whose pictures she bequeathed to the Tate Gallery, including his portrait of herself. Mrs. Hunter, for whom I had a warm regard, used often to engage me to play to her week-end guests, and that is how I came to meet George Moore, Henry James and others.

Despite the vast difference in our ages, George Moore and I became quite comradely and would often go for walks together and discuss literary matters. It so happened that he thought well of my book *The Philosophy of Modernism*, and I suppose on that account he did not look upon me as a nitwit. He was writing his book *The Brook Kerith* at the time, and had already envisaged how it was to end. Yet when I diplomatically pointed out that the proposed ending was too sensational and melodramatic, with remarkably good nature he finally agreed with me and altered his scheme, though I daresay he would have done so in any case.

There was much of the *enfant terrible* about George Moore, and Mrs. Hunter had to be very careful about the selection of his fellow guests. I remember her saying on one occasion: 'Now George Moore, you can't come next week-end because I have invited Alice Meynell [the poetess] and you'll shock her'. And doubtless he would have done, for he sacrilegiously dismissed all Catholics as 'people who believed that God could be turned into biscuits', – the poetess being an especially devout Catholic herself. His summing up of certain novelists was equally ruthless. To Conrad's books he referred as 'the wreckage of Stevenson floating in the slops of Henry James', and for Hardy he had not a good word to say at all.

About his love affairs I found him curiously unreticent. One of our fellow guests was a certain titled woman well known in Society. 'In our younger days', he informed me, 'she let me go to bed with her. But only on condition that I would not actually commit adultery with her.'

Henry James I did not meet often but heard many of his *bons mots* from some of his associates. Personally, although I felt drawn to him in that he radiated kindness, I nonetheless found him rather heavy going, for he talked in such a slow, impressive manner and with so many parentheses that he never seemed to get to the end of his long phrases. Apropos which, when in 1921 I was engaged to play at a large girls' college in America he had recently visited, the Headmistress told me an amusing story. She had asked him to say a few words to the girls, but he had got so entangled in one of his endless sentences that he simply couldn't extricate himself, and there were titters. Suddenly she hit on the idea of clapping so as to start a round of applause, whereupon he had bowed and smiled graciously as if he had made a wonderful speech. I recall another story about him. At an evening party an intense society woman had pushed herself forward and posed the ridiculous question: 'Now tell me, Mr. Henry James, what do you *really* think of Life?' To which he had answered with a great deal of hemming and hahing and much impressiveness: 'Life . . . my dear Madam

. . . if so I may call you . . . is . . . the . . . er . . . *pre dicament*
which er . . . precedes . . . death!'

Two other distinguished men of letters with whom I had
become acquainted were Arnold Bennett and H. G. Wells. A
greater contrast between Wells and Henry James can hardly be
imagined. Outwardly there was nothing the least impressive
about H.G., who was what on first meeting one might have
called 'a dear, unassuming little man'. He had a kindly, genial
face and a high-pitched emasculated voice almost verging on
falsetto. And yet when one talked with him, what a brain he had!
I had stayed with him when he lived at Sandgate near Folke-
stone, and was much intrigued to find that he held the same
sort of views on non-jealous matrimony which I had imbibed
from Mrs. Robert Alan Stevenson, mentioned in a previous
chapter. He had already written his book touching on these,
entitled *In The Days of The Comet*, and among other things, we
discussed this novel as we walked by the sea. But I was somewhat surprised at his admission that although theoretically
right, the 'free marriage' idea had its drawbacks as soon as one
tried to put it into practice. I thought he was going to say that
one's wife might 'cut up rough'. But not at all. What he did
say – rather anticlimatically – was: 'The trouble with love
affairs is that they upset one's digestion.'! . . . Nevertheless, from
what I heard later, during the course of his long life his
digestion must have got upset a good many times!

Of Arnold Bennett I have not much to relate. He certainly
did not give the impression of being the fine literary artist he was
when not writing pot-boilers. Even so I found him a very
likeable man, with his slight stammer and un-stand-offish
demeanour. I had been glad of a chance to meet him because
for one thing I wanted to discover if he was one of those writers
who believed in the subjects they chose for their novels. His
book, *The Glimpse*, had especially intrigued me, for it had led
me to suppose that he possessed a certain amount of occult
knowledge. But this he denied. 'I merely thought the idea
would make a good story', he said, 'and that's the only reason

why I used it.' As the book dealt with an experience in the *etheric body*, 'here is an instance', I reflected, 'of an artist being unknowingly impressed to put across an occult fact.'

The last time I saw Arnold Bennett was at a party given by the most notorious 'celebrity collector' in London. I had been bold enough to go to it in a dark plum-coloured velvet dinner jacket, because I disliked being clothed in nothing but black – the colour of gloom and malice. 'I admire your jacket', said Bennett, 'and only wish I had the courage to wear one like it myself.'

CHAPTER XXIX

Mostly about Friends

THE last chapter is so loaded with celebrities that I may be deemed a snob unless I return now to the mention of some lesser fry.

Over a period of years I enjoyed a curious friendship with a maiden lady. She was some twenty-five to thirty years my senior, a plump little woman with silver grey hair, an agnostic, yet at the same time very conventional in many ways. Being a woman of some means, she gave frequent dinner-parties of a very lavish nature, to which she not only invited myself but any *men* friends I cared to bring. With few exceptions all the women one met at her table were of the somewhat ancient variety, or else had been safely married for some time; incidentally, I fear that several of them were 'spongers'.

I possessed a filial affection for Miss S. and our friendship would have been an entirely harmonious one save for the unfortunate fact that she developed a sentimental attachment for me which proved painful for *her* and embarrassing for myself, in that she became fantastically jealous. It all started owing to a silly, mendacious remark on the part of one of her 'spongers'. Miss S. had said: 'I thought Mr. Scott seemed rather depressed this evening' . . . 'But surely you know why that was?' had been the answer. 'It was because he was not sitting next to *you*'. . . This I subsequently heard from the only friends – a married couple – I made through my association with Miss S. . . Needless to say I felt highly indignant with the woman in question, the more so as her fatuous remark was ultimately responsible for the breaking up of our friendship. For Miss S's. sentiments towards me being what they were, when in 1921 I got married, she wrote and told me that she must bid me 'a very sad goodbye'. In vain did my wife write to her saying that she would never intrude herself in any way and that the friendship could continue exactly as before. But Miss S. did not deign to reply. I heard, however, from the friends previously mentioned that she had said: 'If Mr. Scott wanted to give his name to someone, he could have given it to *me*.'!

Meanwhile, so as to be out of London during the war years, she had from time to time taken furnished houses in the country, to which she invited me to stay as long as circumstances would permit. But I may add that there was always a chaperone in one form or another, which struck me as rather superfluous considering by then she must have been well over sixty. It was while staying with her at Goring-on-Sea that I wrote most of my Opera, *The Alchemist*. This was in 1918 when the war was drawing to its close. Some ten years later she died, leaving twelve wills in her house, not one of which was signed. She was a strange character, who professed to like animals, especially parrots, better than humans. I have always thought of her with affection, and wished that our friendship had not come to such a sorry end.

In the summer of 1918 I paid a visit to Harlech, where I shared some apartments with my friend and occult student A. L. Coburn, the American camera-portrait artist and his wife. (I have briefly mentioned him in connection with Lloyd George). The eminent singer, Astra Desmond, was with us that summer – an artist after my own heart because of her remarkable interpretative qualities and her all-round culture. For frankly to confess, the type of vocalist who merely *sings*, however well, is not the type I would select to render my particular genus of songs. That same summer, the large and genial Granville Bantock and his son were among the visitors at Harlech, whilst as a resident there was the inimitable Josef Holbrooke, who, in the numerous letters he wrote to various journals sounded so acrimonious, yet who in personal contact gave quite a different impression, all the violent fulminations being mostly good-natured cantankerousness, and highly entertaining at that.

Last but far from least of the musicians was Eugene Goossens, then still young, yet a fast budding celebrity. He was staying with an elderly communist millionaire (queer combination) named George Davidson who had built himself a sort of neo-mediaeval castle, in which there was a large hall containing an Aeolian organ and a concert-grand piano with a pianola attached on which Coburn would expertly perform. To this hall both villagers and visitors were cordially invited on certain evenings to partake of musical nourishment either provided by Davidson himself (the organ like the pianola could be played mechanically) or by such visiting musicians who cared to give the guests 'a treat'. As I was fond of improvising on the organ, my services were often in demand, though I hardly think the improvisations merited the blush-raising compliment which Eugene Goossens has since paid them in his book *Overture And Beginners*. But then he has always been very generous about my works, and I think it was he who originally referred to me as 'The Father of British Modern Music'.

At George Davidson's 'castle' there were occasional evenings for discussion, during which G.D. himself would expound his communistic (or were they then called bolshevist?) doctrines. One evening the irrepressible Holbrooke retorted: 'If you believe in all that stuff, why don't you give all your money away and live like a poor man?' Whereupon the enraged Davidson went over to him and hissed in his ear: 'You go to hell, sir!' . . . Still, to do him justice, G.D. in many ways lived up to his tenets. He adopted twelve poor children, had them living in the castle, and gave them an excellent education. All domestics he called 'helpers', and he disapproved of every sort of game on the ground that it was *competitive!* He had an essentially kind heart, though an intolerant mind. He was a rabid agnostic, and if anyone postulated that there might be an after-life he became acrimonious. Nevertheless, when my friend Coburn and one or two others suggested that I should read a paper one evening on Occultism, he raised no objections, sat and listened, then scathingly dismissed the whole thing as 'very amusing'.

Soon after the war ended he went to the South of France where he bought a half-built chateau near Cannes, had it completed according to his own ideas, and lived there for the rest of his life. He was extremely hospitable, and after my marriage, invited my wife and myself, together with our baby daughter and nurse, to stay with him several winters in succession. How the priests contrived it I never heard in detail, but anyhow, after his death a chapel was erected in his grounds and called *Chapelle St. George!* His hatred of religion during his life failed to save him from this 'indignity' when he had passed into the Beyond!

George Davidson displayed that curious admixture of credulity and scepticism which characterises so many of his ilk. He had a very poor opinion of human nature, yet believed that the adoption of Soviet Bolshevism (already overthrown, by the way) would put all things right. Naïvely he failed to see that lust for power, national vanity and the many other concomitants of power-politics would constitute the very obstacle to that desideratum.

I was in London when the war ended in 1918, and I remember that in one of the evening papers HANG THE KAISER! appeared in huge letters; as if that would have been any compensation for all the maimed and slaughtered. Incidentally, I heard later from a German friend 'in the know', that the Kaiser had never wanted the war, and after having been forced to sign the Declaration had dashed the pen to the ground in rage and disgust. The 'merchants of death' of course had made enormous fortunes, and so had others. While our soldiers were being killed at the Front there had been scandalous profiteering at home. Comparatively speaking, I myself had been lucky, for I had only lost one relative and one lovable friend and musical admirer (Irish) whose naïve egotism and inoffensive hypochondria had been a continual source of amusement to most of his associates. When the war started he had recently got married, but his father, an aged, retired Colonel, had told him; 'If you don't join up, you *will* be a poltroon'; – and not being 'a poltroon' he had met with an untimely end. I owe to him an alteration I made in my song *Lullabye* before publication, and which I think improved that trifle to some extent.

The ending of the war brought for me a happy reunion with my friend and publisher Herr Willi Strecker, who at his own request had been interned for two years at Alexandra Palace in company with two thousand waiters and hairdressers! He had lived in England for some years in connection with the house of Schott & Co. in London, but during the first half of the war, neighbours had become so increasingly spy-suspicious and unpleasant, that he thought internment was the only solution to his difficulties.

Soon after the ending of hostilities he returned to his native land to live there permanently. This was unfortunate for me, for I think, what with his charm and dynamic personality, had he remained in England he would have successfully used his efforts to obtain more performances of my larger works in my own country. As it was, he had to confine his endeavours to getting hearings of them abroad, which was no easy matter seeing that the attitude taken by the press was anti all music that was not German. Even so, apart from smaller works, he nearly got a performance of my Opera *The Alchemist*, in Wiesbaden, together with my Ballet, *The Incompetent Apothecary* – but the whole scheme was frustrated because the Opera-house was all but burnt down. However, he did in the end get the Opera produced, minus the Ballet, in Essen, where it was given three performances and then no more because of the antagonism of the papers. Considering that only the previous week Herr Felix Wolfes, the fine conductor there, had produced Debussy's *Pelleas*, this was too much for the German people to stand! and all the vials of journalistic wrath were poured on to the management for its 'unpatriotic behaviour'.

Even Art is not free from the taint of politics.

CHAPTER XXX

I Meet a Remarkable Seer

Around 1919–20 I made, through the theosophist and psychic consultant Robert King, a contact which was to have a very marked effect on my inner life and in many ways on the course of events. King had said to me: 'If you want a nice place to go to for week-ends or longer, I have some friends named Chaplin who run a sort of rest-house at Crowhurst near Hastings. I often go there myself, and it would be very pleasant if you came too. Mrs. Chaplin has remarkable psychic gifts.'

As the result of this recommendation I went frequently to stay at *The Firs*, till Mrs. Chaplin died, and her husband soon after her. She was a most lovable and loving little woman, between fifty and sixty, with a benign, youngish face, silver hair, and despite poor health, a vivacious manner. When Robert King had spoken highly of her psychic gifts he had voiced less than the truth, for what with her wide range of clairvoyant faculties, she turned out to be the most accomplished seer I had ever met. Unlike some clairvoyants and clairaudients, there was never anything extravagant or fantastic about her findings and assertions, none of which were coloured by her own moods or personality. Moreover, as I was soon to learn, she was a very fine medium, not for disembodied entities, like most mediums, but for the Master K.H. with whom she had been in touch almost since her childhood, albeit without knowing his identity. This she had only discovered in later life by what seemed like sheer chance. As far as I remember of what she told me, she had met a lady – I presume a theosophist – who was wearing a locket from which such powerful magnetism emanated that she had asked if she might see what it contained. When it was

7a. Portrait of myself, aged 52, by George Hall Neale. (Bequeathed by his widow to the National Portrait Gallery, at the Committee's request.)

7b. Eastbourne, 1958. (*From left*) Percy and Ella Grainger, Eugene Goossens, Marjorie Hartston Scott, and myself.

8. Myself, aged 71, at our first abode in Eastbourne, sharing a quiet moment Mira, one of our cherished Siamese cats.

shown to her (it contained a miniature) she exclaimed: 'Why, that is the Being I have been in touch with for years. Who is he?' Whereupon she was told: 'That is my Master, the Mahatma Koot Hoomi, or as we call Him, Master K. H.'* I may add here *en passant* that portraits of The Masters – though not very good ones – are hanging in what is called The Shrine Room at the Theosophical Society, hence the owner of the locket would have known from one of these whose likeness she was wearing. It is probable that she had had the miniature copied from one of the portraits, for Masters do not usually supply their pupils with such tokens! nor do they even bother to disclose their names. A High Initiate is discernible by the dazzling radiance of his aura, and what his name may be is considered of minor importance; though his pupils usually find it out in an indirect way in the end, unless for some reason he wishes otherwise.

Nelsa Chaplin also possessed astonishing psychometrical powers; given an object, she could at once correctly relate its history; given a letter she sensed up the feelings and character of its writer. For fun I once gave her a letter to psychometrise from my sentimental friend Miss S. (Miss S.'s letters were always very formal and began 'Dear Mr. Scott'). The moment Mrs. Chaplin had it in her hand she burst out laughing. 'I suppose you've guessed that the old lady is madly in love with you?' she said.

Her clairvoyance was such that she could see disembodied entities as easily as normal persons can see embodied ones, and clairaudiently she could hear all that they said. She was frequently in telepathic communication with Master K.H. and could by reason of her clairaudience transmit any messages or instructions from him to lesser pupils or disciples. Often he would appear to her in one of his *subtler bodies* – roughly stated, in spirit form – then she could of course see him as well as hear his words. Sometimes we would be discussing some obtruse philosophical problem, when suddenly she would break off and

*In this connection a book is of interest: *The Unfinished Autobiography of A. A. Bailey*, (Lucis Press).

F

say: 'Here is Master to solve it for us.' And then he would enlighten us in a few well-chosen words.

Robert King had referred to *The Firs* as a sort of rest-house, but it was much more than that; it was a house in which people received treatment for their various ailments, some of them of a deep-seated and intractable nature, and quite a number of them due to obsession. As Mrs. Chaplin could see the obsessing entities, she knew, with her husband's help, how to deal with them . . . Mr. Chaplin himself (Alec) gave a specific kind of colour-therapy, into which Master K.H. had initiated him. The patient was ordered to lie on a couch in a dark room, and then certain colours from a lamp would successively be projected upon him (or her). But the efficacy of the treatment was due to the fact that Mr. C. would actually *think* the indicated colours into the patient. And how efficacious this unusual method proved, I myself came to experience.

Owing to the worry of the war years I had developed an obstinate form of eczema, and also had at intervals been assailed with a mysterious and very severe pain in my side which used to incapacitate me for whole days or more. Both these troubles, which had not yielded to medical treatment, Alec Chaplin cured in a matter of weeks.

And yet, ill-fated man! he was one of those physicians who could cure others but not himself. He had been among the original experimenters with X-rays and had got burnt, irreparable damage having been done to his stomach. He had already had one serious operation, and was eventually doomed to die after a third and worse one. Meanwhile he carried on his work of service to his Master and to suffering humanity as best he could.

One met a curious assortment of people at *The Firs*, among them theosophists who thought themselves on that account to be very advanced souls, and who fancied they had (or pretended to have) psychic powers which, if the truth be told, existed solely in their own imaginations. I recollect one self-indulgent woman who, whenever Chaplin forbade certain foods which she happened to like, would calmly inform him the next day that in the night 'her Master' had appeared to her and had counteracted his orders. One day this same woman invited Nelsa Chaplin into her bedroom for a 'serious talk', and having got her there solemnly said, 'We must both kneel. The Virgin Mary is present.' It seems needless to add that Mrs. C., who was much amused, could see neither The Virgin Mary nor any other Mary; in fact there were no spirits present at all. . . Not that I wish to give the impression that all theosophists I met at *The Firs* were like this silly, ingenuous woman, for some of them were sincere, sane and charming people. On the other hand, several of them were very conventional, narrow-minded souls who seemed to go through life in a state of chronic disapproval; which caused us some amusement, Mrs. Chaplin herself being endowed with a keen sense of humour, an attribute which they all too obviously lacked.

I was able to do a certain amount of work at *The Firs*, albeit not actual composing, but the orchestrating of such works as were ready for that laborious though interesting process. Mrs. C. was intensely musical, and with her clairvoyant vision could see the colours and thought-forms which the various types of music produced. This was of course for me especially interesting, and although I had no means of proving the truth of her findings, I was content to take them on trust, knowing her to be the kind of seer who never made extravagant statements just for effect. Among the well-known composers, those, she told me, who produced the most brilliant colours and thought-forms were not the so-termed classical composers, but the more modern ones such as Wagner, Debussy, Ravel and Scriabın.

There was a grand piano, of sorts, in the lounge, on which after the evening meal I used frequently to improvise in the then modern style for her benefit. I say for her benefit, for she used to suffer periodically from extremely severe and incapacitating headaches which, strange to relate, my improvisations had the power to dispel. Within a few moments of my starting to play she would go off into *samâdhi* (super-conscious trance) and would remain in that state until the music ceased, after which she would gradually come to, completely refreshed and with no trace of a headache left. So as to help her I would often make these improvisations last as long as forty minutes on end. But care had to be taken to prevent her returning too suddenly to normal consciousness, for in that case she got a nasty shock attendant with some very unpleasant consequences. Usually there were fellow guests present to listen to the music, most of whom already knew about Mrs. C.'s 'peculiarities' and hence kept silent for a few moments after I had stopped playing, so as to give her time to emerge from her trance. But when there were new guests, I hit on the device of gradually gliding, as I neared the end of my rhapsodies, into music of a more obvious and Beethovenesque type, whereupon my 'patient' would slowly and peacefully 'wake up' with her face suffused with mirth. Not that she had a special aversion to genuine Beethoven, but his music neither sent her into *samâdhi*, nor had it any therapeutical effect.* All the same, I am sure that many of her more stodgy guests would have preferred me to treat them to Beethoven or Mozart rather than to the 'incomprehensible stuff' with which I assailed their ears, even though, as she told me, it was doing them good and helping to break down some of the hard outlines of their auras, hard auric outlines denoting conventionality and stodginess.

Although I visited *The Firs* several times before my American tour in 1920–21, it was not until my return to England that I made my first conscious contact with Master K.H. But prior to the tour I did meet and form a friendship with the novelist who was subsequently to become my wife. Master K.H. was also *her* Master.

*I have dealt with the effects of Beethoven's music in my book, *Music, its Secret Influence throughout the Ages*. (The Aquarian Press).

CHAPTER XXXI

American Tour: I Join the Tantrik Order

B^Y my fortieth year my publishers thought I had become sufficiently famous (!) to warrant the American tour. Mr. Elkin had a representative in New York who undertook to look after my interests and to see that I was not taken advantage of by unscrupulous managers. He was a *distingué* but uncompromising Scotsman named George Maxwell, who made the sweeping assertion that all concert agents in America were dishonest, but that at any rate he had picked for me the best of a bad bunch – which was not saying much. As for friends over there, I had Percy Grainger and his mother, who had settled in New York some years previously, Grainger having become an American citizen.

I will not weary the reader with details of my tour. Suffice it to say that in various important towns I played my Piano Concerto, conducted my *Two Passacaglias*, and gave recitals of my piano works, having sometimes had a singer to sing my songs and at other times been obliged (minus the singing) to do all the work myself. I also gave a few lectures in clubs, on matters pertaining to music, with I think a little Occultism thrown in. Canada also figured in my itinerary, and I was amused to find that in that country I was expected to begin all my recitals with the National Anthem, into which, by the way, I was *enfant terrible* enough to introduce alien harmonies. On the whole the press was very kind to me, and in some places gave me more praise than I think I deserved, and certainly more than I received in my native land.

What struck me about the Americans of those days was their intense love of the personal. I was constantly confronted with people who would come up to me and say: 'I am now going

to ask you a very personal question. . . . .' an importunity I
found so embarrassing that I did not know how to cope with
it. In consequence George Maxwell when writing to Mr. Elkin
remarked: 'The trouble with Scott is that he does not suffer
fools gladly.' Maybe, yet no one suffered fools less gladly than
Maxwell himself. When young music students or teachers
would enter his office and ask: 'Say, Mr. Maxwell, can you get
us an autographed photo of Cyril Scott?', he would retort, 'Do
you imagine he keeps a pet photographer and ten secretaries
to cope with your demands?'

It is one thing to be impressed by a country but another to
feel comfortable there. I had only been in the States a short
while when I began to get the curious feeling as if all sense of
poetry in my being had been stifled forever. This may sound
fantastic; yet strangely enough, on my return to England, my
clairvoyant friend Mrs. Chaplin told me I had come back with
a sort of film over my aura. However, not being aura-sighted,
that conveyed little to me. I only know that it took me quite a
time before I could see any beauty or poetry in anything
again. . . But this is merely by the way; for film or no film, it
had not prevented me from being drawn to many of the
charming, warm-hearted Americans I had met.

One thing I did find very gratifying was the absence of any
stinting of money for adequate rehearsals of orchestral works,
and consequently I got very good performances. There was
nothing of what my Swiss friend Hans Lüthy had called 'the
usual English slipshod manner', two rehearsals having to suffice.
In fact, whenever I attend a rehearsal of one of my orchestral
items in England – a rare occurrence – I feel uncomfortable and
chary of stopping the conductor to point out where I would
have it different, for all the while I am conscious of what seems
like an incessant battle against time. In America I was not
harassed by such considerations, and so rehearsals were not a
torment but an interesting experience.

To deal with this battle against time, Percy Grainger's
injunction, 'Make orchestration fool-proof', is all very well up

to a point in *theory*, but it does not always work out in practice. For instance, although he had selflessly spent hours trying to make my *Festival Overture* fool-proof, he could not reckon with the extraordinary acoustic properties of certain halls, the Albert Hall in particular, with its ear-drum shattering pipe organ. Thus, when that Overture was performed at The Proms, at a given moment there was a terrific blast from the organ, drowning the entire orchestra, which ruined the whole balance of the work. Had there been time at rehearsal to experiment, this need not have happened. The trouble is, that in attempting to improve the acoustics of the Albert Hall the outcome has been that the conductor on his rostrum can hardly hear the organ at all, however loud it plays, and so he has no means of gauging its effect. Nevertheless the blame was put on me, the composer, for having written a badly constructed work.

But to revert to America. My tour proved both financially, and if I may say so, artistically a gratifying success. Even so, when later on I was asked to return and make a still more extensive tour, I declined on the grounds that it would interfere for too long with my creative work. It is true that I did have hopes of returning there someday, yet not for professional purposes, but to see again the Tantrik guru, Dr. P. A. Bernard, I had been privileged to contact through one of his pupils who, during the war, had visited England and given some lessons in physiological Yoga.

Apropos which: one day two detectives appeared at my house and asked me to present myself at Scotland Yard, where the then Chief of Police wished to see me. Wondering what misdemeanour I had unwittingly been guilty of, I presented myself as requested. I was then asked what I knew of a certain person named Florin Jones, to which I replied that I knew nothing to his discredit. Whereupon it transpired that the most astonishing and obscene misconstruction had been put upon his activities, that without any trial he had been placed in a cell, had been deprived of his belongings and then deported as an undesirable alien, and even possibly a spy!

The reason for this was that among his possessions had been found some rectal dilators, which are used in physiological Yoga and, incidentally, also by some naturopaths and osteopaths. But seeing they have a rather phallic appearance, the use to which the unfortunate F.J. was alleged to have put them is not politely repeatable here. Further, there is an exercise against constipation which consists in gyrating the abdomen; and this was alleged to be nothing less than the *danse du ventre*. Finally, the Chief of Police, eyeing me severely, said: 'Are you aware that this man blackmailed a lady to the tune of two hundred pounds?' – and not being aware of anything of the sort, I told him so. I afterwards heard from the lady in question, whom I happened to know, that she had *given* him that sum towards the acquiring and furnishing of premises for the holding of classes in Yoga, about which she was enthusiastic, and as for the blackmail, it was sheer nonsense. Needless to say I felt indignant about the whole business, and with D.O.R.A. which made such a thing possible; the more so as Florin Jones had taught me some very beneficial Yoga.

He had promised me that when I came to America he would introduce me to his guru, Dr. Bernard, who lived at Nyack near New York; and he did not go back on his word. . . .

As already implied, the Doctor taught Tantrik Yoga, a combination of Monism and Physiological Yoga. He gave his talks in what was ostensibly a Country Club, but was really his Ashram. I never met a man with such boundless energy. He would start the talks about 8 or 9 p.m. and would continue sometimes for three hours, only to appear fresher at the end than at the beginning. He had an astonishing flow of language, and interlarded his discourses with numerous witticisms and amusing stories, many of them even ribald. He maintained that Nature rightly contemplated was never indecent, hence that prudery, being a wrong attitude to Nature, was a form of indecency. His pupils told me that he could hold his breath for ten minutes at a time and go off into *samâdhi*. To demonstrate the science of Yoga he had on one occasion simulated death before forty physicians and surgeons, many of whom were professors from the various schools of Medicine. (I possess a reproduction of a photograph of him to all appearance dead, and surrounded by the doctors). I was told that the simulation had been so perfect that they had become alarmed at a given point and had begged him to desist. On another occasion, to prove the power of mind over matter (although he never drank alcohol and it was forbidden to bring any into the Club) he had drunk a whole bottle of neat whiskey at one go without its having any noticeable effect on him whatsoever. He was a very heavy cigar smoker, yet to prove that he was no slave to the habit would from time to time give it up entirely. Of sleep he never needed more than four hours, and so he got through a prodigious amount of work. When I met him in 1920 he was just over forty, had a perfect physique and fine features, though any one just meeting him casually would not guess from his appearance that he was a 'great Yogi'.

Certainly he did not behave like a 'holy man', for when approached by people who were not sincere he would behave in a very boorish manner so as to put them off, or else he would tell them quite bluntly that they were no use to him at all. . . . For him an essential qualification was what he called 'the right heart-attitude'; persons with brains but little heart he would not accept as pupils. He was impatient of all conventionality and Pharisaism and would shock conventional people un‧mercifully. Although an American himself, albeit of French-Canadian extraction, he had a poor opinion of American ethical standards, which he maintained were of a very low order indeed. *Au fond* he was unusually controlled in every way, but if one of his pupils displeased him he could fake up a most frightening display of anger, though I personally never witnessed one of these exhibitions. To the contrary, with me he was always very amiable and inspired my admiration and affection.* I met of course many of his pupils, both men and

*My friend Sir Paul Dukes devotes a chapter to Dr. Bernard in his impressive book *The Unending Quest*.

F*

women, and can truthfully say that they were sane, balanced and tolerant-minded persons, with whom it was a pleasure to associate; for Dr. Bernard would brook no cranks and emotional personality-worshippers among his *chelas*. Some of them were married, as was he himself, celibacy not being expected of Tantriks. For his wife, *neé* Blanche De Vries, who subsequently visited me in London, I had and still have a sincere regard, though unfortunately our friendship can now only be conducted through correspondence. Dr. Bernard I did not see again after 1921.

So much then for the story of how I came to join the Order of Tantriks, and if it amused me to mystify people by adding T.O. after my name, I am entitled to do so. But seeing that I have no relish for any sort of name-embellishments where I personally am concerned, I resist the temptation.

CHAPTER XXXII

I Leave U.S.A....
more Data about the Masters

I contacted many charming and hospitable people in America and also in Canada, but when it came to being fêted, I realised that I was quite hopeless as a human lion. I remember one afternoon a party at which I had to shake hands with three hundred people – a most embarrassing and futile ordeal for me! and for them, what purpose did it serve? All I could do was to smile, and all they could do was to say, 'Pleased to meet you, Mr. Scott', the polite and stereotyped phrase. Occasionally I got phone calls asking me to lunch or dinner. Sometimes the wording struck my English mind as so unusual that I remember it still. Seeing that I was announced to play in a certain town, one effusive lady rang me up, invited me to a meal and added: 'I am sure I shall enjoy you, Mr. Scott, and you will enjoy me'.

Despite their democratic principles, many Americans are not free from snobbishness. I was told that I must always stay at the best hotels, as it would look bad for one of my position (!) to do otherwise. Nevertheless, I disobeyed this advice when I went out to Nyack to be with Dr. Bernard and his pupils. I then stayed in a small hotel – perhaps there were no others – and I recollect that one night a curious thing happened. I was on my way to my room, when passing one of the other bedrooms, I heard a very foreign female voice say: 'I luf you to distraction!' A moment later there was a loud and ominous bump on the floor as if somebody had fallen out of bed. Having divested myself of my overcoat and jacket, I was just on my way to the wash-place, when suddenly a large, fleshy woman, enveloped solely in an eiderdown, appeared before me, and in a most imperious manner demanded; 'Wherre is numberr fourrteen?' . . . . 'I'm sorry', I said, 'but I don't happen to know'. . . .

'Wherre is numberr fourrteen?' she insisted in a still more imperious manner. 'I really don't know', I answered, 'but I think it may be round the passage to the left.' Thereupon she turned on her heel and was gone. I have since drawn my own conclusions regarding this incident, though they may not be the right ones.

Apart from this one hotel 'adventure' I had no others; yet, what with the long-distance travelling and the almost constant living in hotels, I was very glad after six months of rush and nervous tension to bid goodbye to America and embark again for home.

Before going to the United States I had lived entirely alone for some months, the friend with whom I had shared the little house in London having got married. But I had a housekeeper who came in daily for a few hours to cook my lunch and do for me generally. Prior to coming home I had notified her as to the time of my arrival. But to my dismay I found on entering the house that she had committed suicide. I discovered her wrapped up in my eiderdown with the gas-tube in her mouth. The poor soul had left me a pathetic note and a number of pawn tickets, having got herself into money difficulties and pawned my clothes. It was a far from pleasant home-coming, and of course I was faced with having to attend the inquest. I had liked the good woman and was much upset at her tragic end.

Mrs. Chaplin, my highly clairvoyant friend, happened to be staying in London at the time, and when I gave her the news, the first thing she did was to burst out laughing. Then, controlling herself, she got into *rapport* with the spirit of the unfortunate woman, who told her that at first she had regretted her foolish act, but was pacified and peaceful after she realised I had forgiven her. 'But why of all places did you go and do it in Mr. Scott's house?' my friend asked her. 'Because I had been so happy there', came the answer. Whereupon Mrs. C. had to burst out laughing again, for it seemed such a curious way of repaying what she apparently considered my good treatment of her. Finally Mrs. C. got into telepathic touch with Master K.H. and heard him say: 'She was sorely tried, so will receive no punishment for what she has done.'. . . The coroner's verdict was 'Suicide while of unsound mind'.

I had come back from America by the Southern route so had not landed at Liverpool. Thus one of my first journeys in England was to visit my mother at Oxton, Birkenhead, where she was still living – more or less alone, for my father had died not long before my American tour.

Since that period in my youthful days when I had shocked and harassed my unfortunate parents by my arrogance and sartorial eccentricities, we had become very good friends, and of course I had often visited them when circumstances permitted. My father's death at seventy-five was due to his having abused his good health and indulged in strenuous activities quite unsuited to a man of his age. In consequence he had injured his heart, and for some time previous to his passing was subject to agonising bouts of *angina pectoris*. Often have I thought that if only I had then possessed the biochemic knowledge I do now, I might have saved him much suffering and prolonged his life. And yet, regarded from the occult stand-point, a man (of the evolved type) dies when his ego decides that he has lived long enough in his present incarnation and that his work is done. Then he may be prompted to do something unwise which brings about his demise. And that is precisely what happened in my father's case. But at least I had the satisfaction of knowing that, whilst I could not help him physically, I had been able to help him spiritually, seeing that a few years before he passed over I had contrived to interest him in Occultism, which it would seem was the very cult he required to satisfy his spiritual needs. This interest, however, was far from being shared by my mother, who looked upon the whole thing with disapproval, together with anything in the nature of Theosophy or Spiritualism.

Which reminds me that in America I had kept away from any of the Theosophical Lodges. The theosophists at that time

were behaving in an extremely untheosophical manner, instead
of observing the principle of Brotherhood, they were quarrelling
among themselves, and this and that person was angling for
the most prominent position in the Society. It was all very
deplorable, and only went to prove once again that no creed,
however liberal or exalted, will automatically transform the
failings of human nature.

1921 was a momentous year for me; it was in that year that
I made my first conscious contact with Master K.H. and that
I married the novelist, later to become known under the name
of Eunice Buckley.

In a previous chapter I mentioned *The Firs*, where Mrs.
Chaplin and her husband lived, and to which I would often go
for a change from town to country. But so far I have not
mentioned that nearly every Sunday morning Master K.H.
would take control of Mrs. Chaplin for the purpose of giving
guidance and instruction regarding the work she and her
husband were doing, together with a doctor, since deceased. I
would stress, however, that Nelsa Chaplin was no ordinary
medium, and that she was never controlled by what are termed
spirits, but only by the Master K.H. and at times by the Master
known to Occultists under the name of Master Jesus, He being
the Initiate Who in a former incarnation some two thousand
years ago had been overshadowed by the yet greater Initiate we
in the West call The Christ.

Although, when controlled by either of these Masters, Mrs.
Chaplin was in a trance, she could nonetheless remember all
that was said, which is not the case where ordinary mediumship
is concerned. I may, though perhaps needlessly, add that in no
circumstances did she give seances and take money for her
services as a medium. At such times as either Master K.H. or
Master Jesus wished to speak with some other pupil (though I
prefer the word 'server') who was not one of the trio, then he
would be sent for, and Mr. Chaplin and the doctor would
withdraw.

As already implied, my first interview with Master K.H.

CHAPTER XXXIII

First Interviews with Master K.H.
— My Marriage

IN all my interviews with Master Koot Hoomi, one of the things, apart from his wisdom which has always impressed me, is the elegance of his language and the choice of his words. By which I emphatically do not mean that he talks in a biblical style or 'sermonises'; for *that* he has too much sense of humour, as becomes apparent from his most appealing, whimsical smile.

During my first interview with him, he told me that he had been using my brain for a number of years; in other words, he had been telepathically impressing ideas upon me, both as regards my music and my books. The reader may ask, what right has anyone, Master or whoever it be, to use a person's brain without his consent and without his even being aware of the fact? This question, however, is based on the assumption that the physical body and brain are the *real* man. But the occult truth is that most of us are less than half alive on the physical plane, as we would know for a certainty if we could bring through the memory of our activities on the higher Planes when out of our bodies in sleep. Some people with psychic faculties *can* bring that memory through, but as yet most persons cannot. In any case it is on the other Planes that the Masters contact such persons who are willing to be used by them, though later on, if desirable, a contact can also be made on the earth-plane.

Which reminds me to pass on some information as to why musical composers are not clairaudient in the accepted sense of the word, the reason being that if they could actually hear the music of the higher Planes, they would so despair of reproducing it with the means at their disposal on the earth-plane, that most of them would be discouraged from even making the attempt. Thus, whereas musicians of the better type are receptive to ideas, or what we call 'inspired' and in so far are mediums for the higher Powers, it would not be desirable that they should be otherwise psychic.

In a previous chapter I mentioned that during the first world war I wrote the book *The Initiate* by *His Pupil;* and I have since been amazed to hear of the large number of people that volume has converted to Occultism and belief in The Hierarchy. There is, by the way, an amusing if discreditable story connected with that book as the result of my anonymity; for Mrs. Chaplin informed me that no less than three different people told her that they were its author!

In an *Afterword* to one of the editions of my *Outline of Modern Occultism,* I stated that, although it was my hand which wrote the 'Initiate Series' of books, the material was given to me by someone else whose identity could not be revealed. Even so, I discovered from K.H. that it was he who in the first place had actually prompted me to relate the story of the man I called 'J.M.H.' The Masters had wished to put the books through as an experiment in the hopes that they might bring some enlightenment to many who were groping in darkness. Though the books are very popular among theosophists, I hear that the Society regards them as fiction, on the assumption that no such person as 'J.M.H.' ever existed. Well, it matters not what they believe so long as the books have served their purpose.

I got married in the unlucky month of May! Though had it not been for my Master's wish I would never have got married at all. He did not order me or compel me to marry but I realised that to have refused would have been a folly. The reasons he put forward were ones I had not considered hitherto. In fact, the idea of marriage had always been distasteful to me. I did not consider in-loveness a basis for matrimony, seeing that that state is full of illusions; no one really knows a person with whom he (or she) is in love, he merely imagines he does. As for marrying for the sake of having children, I had no such desire. Further, not being then an old man, I saw no reason for marrying a companion for the purpose of leaving her money; in short, I could find no convincing reason for not remaining an unencumbered bachelor.

Nevertheless, K.H. changed all my preconceived notions. He pointed out that it was not well for a man to live alone, for it was apt to foster selfishness and make him an introvert. Moreover, there was the literary *work;* Rose Allatini (her actual name) was or rather is not only a writer of considerable talent and ability but has a remarkable flair for literary criticism and could pounce on mistakes, oversights, solecisms and lapses of good taste with the eye of an eagle. Finally, there was some karma brought over from our last life together which had to be worked off between us, and if not adjusted in this present incarnation would have to be in the next – so why delay its liquidation? All these appealed to me as sound reasons for marrying Rose, who, likewise being a server of Master K.H. had already given her consent to his suggestion, albeit at some sacrifice to herself.

Incidentally, we both heard through him who we had been in our last life, though I am not prepared to divulge our names. Suffice it to say that neither of us was English, that Rose was an authoress and I a composer and had been one in my previous life. Between my last life and the present one I was only out of incarnation some thirty years, and Rose still less.

It may amuse the reader to know that whereas I derive some pleasure from hearing the works I wrote in my last rebirth, with a few exceptions I am bored by those I wrote in my earlier one. But considering the lot of nonsense talked by some believers in reincarnation who pretend they were kings, queens or similar grandiose personages, the less said about past lives the better. What concerns this story is that Rose and I made what among Occultists is called an occult marriage, and I for one have never regretted it.

I had only been married a few months, when my mother – who was glad to see the end of my bachelordom and had taken to my wife – died of bronchial pneumonia. Yet, in view of her loneliness, I felt glad for *her* sake that she should go. I was, despite all my convictions, much affected at her funeral, and envied my sister who, strange to say, only wept at weddings! 'After all, as an illiterate friend wrote me, 'One only has one mother, hav'nt you?'

Soon after her passing I visited *The Firs*, where Mrs. Chaplin at once got in touch with her – or better, said she came to us – and Mrs. C. could see her clairvoyantly and hear all she had to communicate.* However, as I am not writing a book on Spiritualism and have mentioned her communications in *My Years of Indiscretion*, I will not repeat them here. I will only say that Master K.H. subsequently told me that she was then on a Plane where all genuine thoughts of selfless affection take flower-forms of much beauty, and that being a happy one, I need have no fears about her well-being. This was interesting to me – though it may mean nothing to the reader – because my mother had commented on the astonishing profusion and loveliness of the flowers.

While I was sitting conversing with Mrs. Chaplin, Percy Grainger's mother also appeared in spirit form. I had only seen her a few weeks previously in New York, and then came the news of her tragic death after I had left America, which was of course a great shock to me. In the hopes of it being a little comfort to her son, she asked us to convey a certain message to him, and this I was only too glad to do. But his reactions to my letter were so unfavourable that I wished I had refrained. What so many people do not realise when they feel hurt that a departed and much loved friend or relation should appear to somebody else instead of direct to *them*, is that such appearances would be quite impossible unless they had the faculty to *see*.

* See Appendix II.

CHAPTER XXXIV

Vienna, Germany, Switzerland
and Old Friends

ONE of the first things my wife and I did after our marriage
was to visit Germany, but prior to that, Vienna, where
she had several families of relations. In the home of one of her
specially charming uncles we spent three months. Although
Vienna itself had sadly changed and looked as if paint had
become very scarce, the people were the same genial, friendly,
melody-loving folk, the concerts still excellent and the opera,
as far as I could judge, up to standard. While we were staying
there, two of my more or less major works were performed.
Naturally I renewed my acquaintance with the erstwhile Frau
Gustav Mahler, who since our last meeting had married the
novelist Franz Werfel. The two were so very different in
appearance and personality, that had I not come to believe in
links from past lives the alliance would have seemed incomprehensible. . . . Incidentally, she said I ought to call on the
composer Arnold Schönberg, telling me he would be flattered
by my visit! But as his music had never appealed to me, and I
am no good at paying mendacious compliments, I thought it
best to avoid what might have been an embarrassing interview.
(I have learnt since, through reading her autobiography, that
she had come under the musical influence of Schönberg and his
disciples, since when she found my music 'too refined for her
taste'.).

After leaving Vienna, my wife and I visited, in Cologne, my
old piano teacher Prof. Uzielli and his second wife, who gave
us a heart-warming welcome.

Except for his white hair he was quite unchanged, and as well
turned out as ever. We asked him how he contrived to look so
smart when everything was so outrageously expensive. And he

told us that as most clothes then procurable were largely made of paper, he had had his old suits turned.

By that time my German had got rather rusty, and I made some frightful and distinctly ribald bloomers which caused much merriment. It was the period of the great inflation, but fortunately the 'Frau Professor' had relations and interests in America and so the united couple were not too impoverished. This is more than could be said for the first Frau Uzeilli, whom we visited in Frankfurt, and who insisted on inviting us to supper. Indeed, her circumstances were such that we felt reluctant to eat the meal she had provided. To add to the pathos of it all, one of her sons had lost an eye in the war. And all for what? As the Tibetan Master has pointed out: 'Mankind is concerned with war and with horrible preparations for more war, and is not primarily occupied with that which *causes* war and which, if rightly handled, would prevent war.'

Frau Uzielli's singing career was long since over, and she was giving lessons to indifferent amateurs. That was the last time I saw this fine artiste, this cultured and warm-hearted woman, who had encouraged me so much in my earlier days and helped me to make some of my songs more 'singable'. She died a few years later, having previously taken up Christian Science.

In Mainz I saw, also for the last time, my publisher Geheimrat Dr. Strecker. This extremely handsome, aristocratic and charming man was just convalescing after the amputation of a leg. He himself had retired from the business some time ago, but his sons were carrying it on and having to contend with labour troubles, strikes and disputes of all sorts, to say nothing of the frightful difficulties due to the inflation. We heard that hundreds of respectable and respected old people had been driven to commit suicide, all their savings having become entirely valueless, whilst they themselves were too old to work or quite unable to find any work. Things had come to such a fantastic pass that it required a million-mark note to pay even for a tram-fare. It was all heart-lacerating.

In Berlin I found my old friend Melchior Lechter living in greatly straited circumstances, for nobody had any money to buy pictures, let alone stained-glass windows. The faithful Abigail who had served him for twenty years had had to leave him because he could no longer afford to keep her, and although he still lived in his very ecclesiastical abode, there was now an air of shabbiness about his studio. His health had deteriorated and he suffered much from his heart, but he was still an indefatigable worker. Nor did his condition deter him – his interest in music being as keen as ever – from inviting a number of musical friends to come and hear me give an impression, as best I could on the piano, of my Opera *The Alchemist*, which I had completed during the war. None of his guests displayed the slightest ill-feeling towards me despite what were then recent hostilities. Present on that occasion was the German composer, Richard Wintzer, then acting as music critic on one of the Berlin papers. This unfortunate man had written several Operas, not one of which had been given a performance. On the evening in question I formed a friendship with his talented actress-daughter, who still writes to me after all these years.

Notwithstanding his heart-trouble, Melchior Lechter contrived to live for another sixteen years after our last meeting in Berlin. We had corresponded fairly often in the earlier days of our association, but as he grew old, the labour of writing in his very stylised calligraphy (he wrote entirely in capitals) became too much for him and our correspondence lapsed. He died in Switzerland at the age of seventy-two – and Germany lost another of her great artists.

The mention of Switzerland brings back the memory of the times my wife and I spent in Lausanne. A few years prior to our marriage I had picked up the stitches, so to say, of a very old association, which by now the reader may have forgotten, since it relates to my boyhood and that strange family I lodged with in Frankfurt. I allude to the Seiler menage, Frau Seiler being the selfish and self-dramatising *malade imaginaire* who had demanded that her husband should perform for her the most unpleasant duties of a sick-nurse. Her buxom, auburn-haired daughter had married, as I mentioned, a Monsieur Vohl and had gone to live in the South of France. How some twenty-five years later I discovered they were running a hotel in Lausanne I have forgotten; anyhow, once having heard it, I visited them there, became so friendly with them both that subsequently my wife and I would from time to time put up at their hotel to enjoy their company, and the delights of Switzerland. Old Frau Seiler, having lost her accommodating husband, was living with them and had had to pull herself together and conduct her bodily affairs like a normal person, for her quick-tempered, rather domineering daughter would stand no nonsense in *her* hotel. Nor, being both a very religious and very jealous woman, would she, unless obliged to, stand any moral laxity on the premises. Nevertheless, when occasionally the Chief of Police would appear in mufti with a pre-possessing young lady and engage a room for the afternoon where they could 'have a rest' as he put it, she had diplomatically to suppress her moral principles, otherwise, as she somewhat shame-facedly explained to us, he could easily have made things very unpleasant.

Meanwhile her own husband, unbeknown to her but not to me, was conducting a love-affair with a girl who was a relation of one of her old friends, and whom she was more or less be-mothering. She had short-sightedly made the mistake of going away to England with old Frau Seiler for a six-weeks holiday, leaving the attractive young woman to keep the romantic and poetic-looking Mr. Vohl company in her absence. And of course the inevitable happened; both parties had fallen violently in love with each other, and this, despite the fact that Mr. V. was already in the throes of an intrigue with a Swiss woman in the vicinity.

Yet to do him justice, my friend was not a libertine or a sensualist, but a warm-natured, affectionate individual whose misfortune it was, in the circumstances, to have a physical aversion to fat women. What he had not had the *nous* to foresee when he married the already buxom Frl. Seiler was that in a few years her buxomness would surely develop into something more formidable, and so he was one of the innumerable victims of Nature's unkindness to many members of the fairer sex. I had tried to instil into Mme. Vohl's jealous head that even conjugal jealousy was an ignoble and childish passion, but although she was prepared, while continuing her church-going and other observances, to accept some of my theosophical tenets, when it came to asking her to tolerate husbandly infidelities, that was going too far! and she was or pretended to be shocked on moral and religious grounds. Thus, when she discovered her husband's *amour*, both she and her pietistical old mother rounded on me for corrupting him with my 'immoral' ideas, and, as they put it, for condoning his disgraceful conduct: for they guessed rightly that he had confided in me, and it was no use denying the fact. 'You have not been a good friend to me in taking his part,' said the much hurt Mathilda, as I had come to call her: 'You ought to have told him that he was doing something very wrong indeed, and if he wouldn't listen, then come and told *me*.' As if he would have listened in any case!

It was all rather naïve, for apparently she had expected me to behave like 'a dirty little schoolboy sneak' and betray her husband's confidences. Still, it must be said in her favour that when she realised the dilemma in which I had been placed, being really a charitable-hearted and loving soul, she forgave me and allowed the whole affair to make no difference to our friendship. But as for the young lady, she was banished back to her home in England. After seeing her off at the station, the much upset Mr. Vohl came to my bedroom, where with tears in his eyes he lamented over the cruelty of Fate and over the lack of wifely understanding!

All this had happened before my marriage, and by the time my wife and I went to stay with the ill-assorted couple, the sentimental though endearing Mr. V. was in the thick of another intrigue, though about this one his wife was not only left thoroughly in the dark, but, to put it vulgarly, got hold of quite the wrong end of the stick.

Among the Vohl's acquaintances there was a somewhat round-faced, attractive German girl, to whom, by the way, I always referred as 'Lovely Cat', and who was married to an unattractive Frenchman of lanky stature. This couple would often drop in at the hotel after the evening meal. Mme. Vohl liked the girl, and believing that Mr. V. had been behaving himself with propriety for quite a while, and in any case that the girl was safely married, did not discourage the visits. All went quite smoothly along moral and conventional lines until one day, getting my confiding friend alone, 'Lovely Cat' confessed to him that she had badly lost her heart in his direction. This was enough to set his inflammable nature alight, and since the confession, the pair had been carrying on a most passionate affair without the knowledge of Mme. Vohl or the girl's lanky husband.

I must confess that instead of being shocked at these goings-on, both my wife and I were naughtily amused, though we hoped that the affair would fizzle out before the strait-laced Mathilda got to hear of it; otherwise once again there would have been a very unpleasant situation to face. I asked my friend how he contrived to conduct the intrigue so secretly, considering his jealous wife always demanded to know where he was going, where he had been, what he had been doing and so on. But he told me that it was all quite simple; he would merely tell her he had shopping to do, or was going to his Freemason Lodge, when actually he would go to the girl's flat while the husband was pursuing his profession.

When my wife and I visited the Vohls again the following year, we were almost afraid to mention 'Lovely Cat' to Mathilda in case the whole intrigue had been discovered. But our fears were quite unwarranted, for what *had* been discovered was something very different. With a great display of righteous indignation, the good Mathilda informed us that 'Lovely Cat's' husband had taken up with a typist.

'Just think of such a thing!' she exclaimed; 'And there is that nice girl not able to do anything about it. And we thought Monsieur B – was such a decent, good man!'

The irony of it was that her husband was still clandestinely misconducting himself with the 'fallen idol's' wife. When my memory harks back, as it often does, to those two souls and their predicament, the more does the convention of conjugal jealousy seem incompatible with that true emancipation towards which we hope the human race is evolving, when, incidentally, the seventh Mosaic Commandment may be seen in a different light. For in view of what has emerged from history and study, would not a much more rational interpretation of that rather ambiguous Commandment be, 'Thou shalt not adulterate *the race* – that is to say, by mating with units of other races? But interpret it as we will, the fact remains of course that conjugal fidelity is desirable; and fortunate are those married couples who love each other both spiritually, mentally and physically.

My final sojourn with the Vohls, by the way, was in 1938. They had given up the hotel and, having weathered all their matrimonial storms, had settled down into a peaceful Darby and Joan relationship, completely devoted to one another. They were both over eighty but still mentally alert. I asked my friend if he ever saw 'Lovely Cat'? 'She sometimes comes round to have a talk,' he replied. 'But she has got fat and vulgar.' 'No more affairs for you now?' I asked with a twinkle. '*Nein*,' he said (we often spoke German) '*jetzt geht es nicht mehr.*'

His wife died in the early years of the war. '*Die Tildschen ist eingeschlafen*,' he wrote. 'My life is no use to me any more. When one loses the companion who has shared all one's ideas and one's interests, there is nothing left to live for.' He died some two years later. Both he and his wife had been loyal and loving friends to me.

CHAPTER XXXV

Music and Occultism: My Opera in Essen

IT was during the 'twenties that I wrote the book, *Music: Its Secret Influence Throughout the Ages*.* While my wife and I were staying at *The Firs*, Master K.H. one Sunday intimated that the time had come when it was desirable to make known the esoteric aspects of music, and that The Masters wished to use my pen to that end. 'I will,' he said, 'give the data to "the little one" (as he called Mrs. Chaplin) and *you* will work them out in detail.' Needless to say, Mrs. C. and I were extremely glad to co-operate in this work together, and devoting certain times to it, she would 'listen in' to K.H. while I would write in my notebook what he communicated. I wish to emphasize here that I had previously had no idea about the occult effects of music, and especially the respective effects produced by nearly each composer of established renown.

We learned that by means of a form of wordless suggestion, music acts on the minds and hearts of men; that the celebrated composers had been inspired by The Masters to intensify certain emotions in man, and thus had been instrumental to a large extent in moulding morals and trends of thought. Already centuries ago, Plato, who was an Initiate, had known about the occult effects of the tonal art, hence had he written that styles of music could not be altered 'without disturbing the most important political institutions.' And yet he was only speaking of the comparatively simple music of his own times, therefore how much greater the effects of music as we know it to-day. Handel, Bach, Beethoven, Chopin, Mendelssohn, Schumann, Wagner, Tchaikovsky, Brahms, Debussy, Ravel, and Scriabin had all been used to bring about certain effects desirable for

* The Aquarian Press.

the furtherance of the evolution of the race, even though they had not been aware of the source of their inspiration nor the respective effects that sooner or later would eventuate from their creations. (For instance, the full effects of Wagner's music will not be operative for nearly two hundred years.) This ignorance on their part was not a drawback but an advantage, for had they known what particular effects The Hierarchy wished them to produce, they might have *consciously* tried to produce them and so frustrated true inspiration. If Mendelssohn, for one, had known that his mission was mostly to express and augment the virtue of sympathy, he might have set about deliberately composing what he *thought* to be sympathy-arousing pieces, and in the end merely have engendered an inferior work of art. Only an Initiate of a certain degree knows the effects a given type of music can create, *not* the medium he may inspire to put that music through.

I have mentioned Mendelssohn as the most simple example, most of the other musicians alluded to being much more complex as regards their particular effects, which cannot be enlarged upon in these *Confessions*, having already been dealt with in the book concerned. I would merely point out as a matter maybe of interest to some of my readers, that one of the reasons why many of the great composers had such a struggle to get their music heard and appreciated was due to the efforts and machinations of the Dark Forces. For as soon as the Brothers of The Great White Lodge (The Hierarchy) seek to put across anything, be it music, art, literature or what not for the upliftment of mankind, then the brothers of the Left-hand Path at once endeavour to oppose Them and undo Their work.

The book on the occult influence of music was finally published, and whilst on the whole it received a not altogether unfriendly press, the eminent musical *littérateur* Ernest Newman was able to indulge in an orgy of causticity and fun-poking at its expense. He headed his article 'Pythagoras Dodders', I having mentioned in the book that Master K.H. had been that Sage in a previous incarnation. Although this seemed rather undignified journalism on the part of a man who had written such a masterly biographical book on Wagner, it was more or less to be expected, for I had also mentioned destructive music-criticism as one of the measures employed by the Dark Forces. All the same, I bear no grudge against Mr. Newman, with whom I had been personally acquainted for very many years, and especially as I have heard that a bad review sells a book better than a good one. But whether that be true or not, the book has already gone into several editions, and so I have nothing to complain about.

The facile argument used against the volume was '*post hoc, ergo propter hoc*' (coming after, therefore in consequence, a logical fallacy) which in many cases can be a fallacy itself. How was it possible, and what use, to state the occult effects, say, of the Wagnerian music before Wagner himself existed?! Moreover, what would it have availed to give out the esoteric aspects of music until an increasing interest in Occultism had made a certain number of people ready for such information? The Masters do not waste their valuable time on futilities.

When in 1928 my Opera *The Alchemist* was produced at Essen, we took Mrs. Chaplin with us to Germany, as she was very anxious to hear the work. Some of the singers were hostile to me on national grounds, and the conductor, Felix Wolfes, complained to us after the performance that in consequence they had acted like 'sticks'. There had been difficulties with the translation, much of which had had to be altered before the rehearsals began. I had purposely avoided flowery language when writing the libretto, but the young man who had been engaged by the publishers to translate it, imagined that a libretto *ought* to be of a flowery nature and had tinkered with it accordingly, in many places completely altering the sense. All this meant extra work at the theatre and did not add to my popularity!

At the final rehearsal there was nearly a serious row, though I was not involved in it, and Mrs. Chaplin had to send a mental S.O.S. to Master K.H. to come in one of his subtle bodies and diffuse peace. However, on the evening of the actual performance the audience was friendly and gave the work a good reception, but the singers declined to appear with me to acknowledge the applause.

In Essen originated for me a still-enduring friendship with Hannah Spohr, a descendant of Louis Spohr, the well-known composer. She was at that time Mistress of the Ballet and choreographer at the Essen Theatre, and as she had a hand in the production of my Opera, I saw quite a lot of her and was impressed with the ingenuity and quality of her work. So much so, indeed, that when in 1930 she suggested putting on, in Dortmund to where she had moved, a Ballet of mine with her own 'plot' and choreography, I consented with enthusiasm.

This Ballet had been originally composed at the request of André Charlot – charming and cultured man – for one of his Revues in London during the 'twenties. Being an idealist and a music enthusiast, he wished to introduce into his show an item of a more serious character than is customary in such forms of entertainment. I fear it cost him a lot of money to produce, but, as he generously told me later, 'it had been well worth while'. We called the Ballet *Karma*, in view of its plot. In the 'thirties he commissioned me to write music for another Ballet, this time to Poe's gruesome story, *Dance of the Red Death*, which certainly made a very fine display.

When Hannah Spohr produced my (first) Ballet in Dortmund, I went over for the occasion, and was delighted with her conception of the whole work. But then Frl. Spohr is not only a choreographer but a remarkable dramatist as well, having written in what we call 'the grand manner' a Trilogy – *Animus Universalis* – of outstanding originality and power.

My reception in Dortmund by the press was very different from the one I had experienced in Essen. The leading newspaper gave me a most favourable notice, and what is more, did me the honour of printing an interview with me. One of the things I was asked to elucidate was the reason why the English had so little taste for opera, considering that in Germany even quite small towns had their subsidized opera-house! Precisely – so why *are* we in England so far behind Germans in this respect? The unflattering answer is that we (I must exclude myself) are much more preoccupied with matters of cricket and football than with the fine arts. Are we not even taught already at school to regard games with something approaching reverence? (Curious combination, games and reverence.) However, not wishing to make this damning admission, I fell back on the pretext that perhaps we British had too much sense of humour; which remark merely landed me in a difficulty, for in German there is no exact equivalent for 'sense of humour', nor could my puzzled interviewer see the connection between serious opera and the humorous. I could not very well state in a printed interview that the spectacle of two enormously fat singers embracing each other, or trying to, was apt to strike many Britishers as more ridiculous than emotionally moving! Moreover, not all opera-singers are distortingly fat. And so my interviewer had to fall back on his journalistic inventiveness.

9a. At work in my music room – 1969.

9b. With Marjorie Hartston Scott at our home in Eastbourne.

10. Myself – in the late eighties.

CHAPTER XXXVI

Reflections about Style,
Musical Sensationalism, etc.

ALTHOUGH I have confessed frankly and freely my occult
and other opinions, so far I have not stated my musical
ones – for what they are worth.

Contact with scores of professional musicians of every species
has convinced me that comparatively few of them hold an
unbiased attitude towards music itself. Conductors are apt to
like the kind of music which is the most effective to conduct;
pianists, violinists, cellists and other instrumentalists the works
which are most effective for their respective instruments; and
singers the songs which show them off to the greatest advantage.
I once knew an operatic tenor who declared that one of
Meyerbeer's operas, I have forgotten which, was the finest
opera in existence. When I asked him why he thought so, he
said, because it contains the most effective high C ever written!
In my student days in Frankfurt there was a particularly good
hornplayer. One day, for fun, my professor, Iwan Knorr, asked
him how he liked Wagner. 'Ach', was the reply with a gesture
of disgust, 'no good, no good. He always overworks the horns.'
This was another point of view, but still a biased one.

Thus in the end I have come to the conclusion, despite my
earlier views, that (allowing of course for exceptions) the only
groups of people who listen to music with unprejudiced minds
are the cultured amateurs and the good-music-loving public.
As for composers, they are by no means the best judge of other
composers, and in some cases may even be the very worst.
Chopin disliked Beethoven, and Weber after hearing his 8th
Symphony, said he was ready for the madhouse. My colleague,
Herbert Murrill, at one time Musical Director of the B.B.C. –
he has since died, alas – went so far as to admit that he disliked

all the Teutonic masters, and that virtually every composer between the times of Corelli and Debussy gave him no pleasure. With regard to myself, I must confess that quite a lot of what is rightly accepted as great music frankly bores me. Yet to put me to shame and to prove my point, there is my friend Charles Douglas Stafford, who being one of the best examples of the cultured amateur, can appreciate almost any music modern or ancient that is really good, and who possesses such a comprehensive library of gramophone records, that whenever I spend a week-end with him I have only to ask for whatever I wish to hear, and it is always forthcoming. . . . Of course, the cultured amateur is not to be confounded with those people who say, 'I'm not musical, but I know what I like'; a silly remark presumably meaning, 'I like what I know'. However, this attitude need not detain us.

To pass on to other matters: there being 'nothing new under the sun', I submit that all individual styles are the result of selection, combination and *limitation;* a truism which persons overlook when they unfavourably compare some contemporary composer with master-musicians of the past. Some of them think to rationalize their dislike by dubbing him a mannerist, not realising that the line of demarcation between a stylist and a mannerist is very slender indeed. For instance, Iwan Knorr used to refer to Grieg as a mannerist, yet would have been horrified if I had applied that term to Handel or Bach, even if I had meant it in no derogatory sense. The facts can nevertheless not be denied, for these masters could seldom write even a few bars without resorting to *imitations* or *sequences*, or both. Again, if any contemporary composer used an uncommon chord as frequently as Handel and Beethoven used common ones, he would certainly be called a mannerist by the musical wormhole-seekers. Handel's *Hallelujah Chorus*, for example, consists mostly of common chords, and as for the last movement of Beethoven's 5th Symphony, the vast number of times the common chord of C occurs is a proof of my contention.

But few people notice all these to-day, simply because they

are common chords, because Beethoven wrote them, and because in his day such chords formed, as it were, the groundwork on which musical structure was built. Variety was not achieved through harmonic inventiveness but largely through melody, melodic phrases, rhythm, florid passages and modulative devices. Nowadays (I write in 1959, and in a few years all may be changed again) the common chord is superseded, and many extremist composers resort to unrelieved discordancy, consisting for the most part of *diminished octaves* and *false relations*. They eschew distinguishable melody as something *vieux jeu* and savouring of the now despised 'romantic', whilst discernible modulation is impossible because there is virtually no key from which to modulate into another. These extremists who write what Holbrooke called the 'excruciating type of music' are seemingly just as afraid of beauty and anything approaching charm as were the academics fifty years ago of anything approaching ugliness. The latter were slaves to the musical conventions of *their* times, whereas the former are slaves to the musical conventions of *our* times, the pendulum having swung from musical academicism to musical sensationalism.

The trouble with such music, however, is that, granted a liberal number of discords are necessary for musical expressiveness, continuous discordancy ends in mere monotony and therefore in an unsatisfying work of art. Although monotony may not be disturbing where quite short pieces are concerned, any lengthy composition becomes boring if it lacks adequate contrasts; by which I do not mean merely dynamic ones but, even more importantly, emotional ones. Music which is all head and no heart is as unsatisfying in the long run as music which is all heart and no head, and as practically all the greatest music of the past oscillated between these two qualities, I think it is safe to predict that the greatest music of the future will do likewise.

Meanwhile we have the various schools and fashions, notably the so-termed 'Twelve note music', and the Neo-classic school, which largely consists of writing in the classical style but with

G*

the introduction of alien notes and progressions. This 'old-wine-in-new-bottles' type of music has its admirers, on the other hand there are those whom it merely irritates, because to them it seems little better than a caricature of the classical composers. Yet whichever way one looks at it, the fact remains that any composer who follows the dictates of a given school or fashion, in so far fetters his creative imagination (if he has one) instead of giving it free rein. The truly creative composer is a law unto himself.

As to fashions themselves, they occur when mere cleverness, facility and technical ability preponderate over true inspiration: in other words, when there is a fertility of mediocrity, if the jingle be pardoned. I am not of course suggesting that today the world of music is peopled entirely with mediocrities, for this would be a gross and insulting overstatement. But I do say that intrinsic worth has nothing to do with fashions, and vice versa.

Incidentally, fashions in turn give rise to musicological catch-words. In my young days one such catch-word was 'futuristic', nowadays it is 'romantic', and used in a derogatory sense at that. Its misusers seem to forget that the classical composers had their romantic moments, and even the despised romanticists their heroic ones. The labelling of composers may be an amusement for 'learned idlers', to quote Nietzsche, but it tends to obscure true values, for surely a fine work of art *is* or remains one whatever it may be labelled?

Speaking from the occult angle and the light it throws on present-day musical vogues, there is this to be said to those people who cannot understand why so much modern music is ultra-discordant. Roughly stated there are two types of composers, those who, being inspired by the Higher Powers, help through the medium of music to mould the desirable characteristics of the future, and those who not being thus inspired merely express the characteristics of the present. And as we live in an age of extreme contentiousness, political cruelty (in some countries) fear and terrible unrest, the result, translated into music, is ugliness and cacophony. True, there are still other reasons, but as I mentioned them when writing the book on the secret influence of music, I will not repeat them here.

I have now confessed to some of my musical opinions and it only remains for me to own up to my musical sins, if so they be. First (as already mentioned) I plead guilty to not having 'progressed' with the times; though I cannot thus plead, if I may say so, to not having progressed along the line and within the limits of my own particular idiom – assuming it is conceded that I possess an idiom at all. Secondly, I plead guilty to employing an *uncommon* chord with the same frequency as at one time common chords were used; so anybody can therefore call me a mannerist if so minded. This chord as my groundwork, so to say, would seem to permit of a considerable number and variety of combinations to be built upon it, apart from the fact that it can be used on any of the twelve degrees of the chromatic scale.* Thirdly, I plead guilty to moving my chords and parts in similar motion more often than is considered right and proper, though not to the extent of which I have been accused.

As against all this, I can *not* plead guilty to having *deliberately* attempted to express through the medium of music any occult or mystical facts. If I do possess an individual style, it has, as far as any objective knowledge on my part is concerned, been evolved entirely subconsciously, and is based on no *school* or theory. Had I been asked to express certain emotions or produce certain occult effects, I should not have known how to do so. Nor do I know what sort of occult effects the works I have already composed would produce if given a hearing. I can merely say in this connection that I have been told by Master K.H. – though only fairly recently – that the 'keynote' of the music I am still destined to write will be 'Unification in its widest sense'. Precisely what form that music will take I have no idea, and *can* have no idea until it has been actually written.

As a matter of pure conjecture, I imagine that much of the

* See Appendix V.

music of the future may be relatively simple. My reasons for so thinking are that when music has reached an apex of complexity it has often been followed by a new sort of simplicity, as witness, after the contrapuntal profundities of Bach came the simplicities of Mozart. As for discordancy, music cannot become more discordant than it now is without ceasing to be music at all, hence there is likely to be a swing of the pendulum in the other direction. Further, I think that melody and melodic phrase is likely to play once more an important part in music,* and, in fine, that the days of the glorification of ugliness are numbered. After all, it is comparatively easy to create a new form of ugliness, but it takes a genius to create a new form of beauty – and, I may add, a new and valid form of simplicity.

* See Appendix IV.

CHAPTER XXXVII

Children: Death of Mrs. Chaplin: New Contacts

MASTER K.H., having wished us to have two children, told me that one would be a boy and the other a girl, but he added that for certain reasons he did not propose to divulge in which order they would come. Personally I was indifferent, for it is the ego which counts and not the sex, and I told him so. 'Good! my son,' was his comment. As it turned out, my daughter came first, a fact for which many years later we had reason to be thankful.

Some people seem to be very pleased and proud, like animals, when they have increased the number of their species. I remember one American who came to see us just after my daughter was born, and who said to my wife, 'If I were in your position, I would simply be bursting with pride and gratification!' Poor lady, she was almost bursting as it was, for I have seldom seen a fatter woman. I had a German friend in those days who also seemed to think that parental pride was a commendable emotion. He would suddenly catch up one of his offspring and pressing it to his bosom would exclaim, 'one's own flesh and blood!' Not being especially enamoured of my own personal flesh or blood, these exhibitions used merely to embarrass me. To be fond of one's children is one thing, but to be proud of having produced them is quite another. And for why? – because it is based on a misconception. Nobody can produce a soul, they can only provide it with a temporary habitation, and if they are proud about that, then they must be very vain people!

During the years when my daughter and son were successively on the way, I often found myself depleted and had to go to *The Firs* for treatment. I would not think this worth mentioning did

it not throw some occult light on something which many
husbands may have experienced. When a man now and then
feels off colour during his wife's pregnancy, his condition is
most often put down either to coincidence, sympathy or worry
about her health, all of which assumptions may be wrong or
only true in part. They tend to prevail because as yet the
medical profession does not generally know about the *etheric
double* despite the fact that it is perceptible to clairvoyants, and
with practice to non-clairvoyants by means of the Dr. Kilner
Screens. This subtle body, otherwise called the 'Health Aura' is
very vital, and being of rarefied substance can be drawn upon
by the incoming ego. And so, when a reincarnating soul
appropriates some of its prospective father's so termed *etheric
double*, the latter suffers in consequence until such time as the
lesion has healed up. I myself was fortunate, in that my
clairvoyant friend Mrs. Chaplin could see exactly what had
happened and give me the right form of treatment, and hence
I got over my troubles fairly quickly, but I have known men
who, believing in nothing but what they could see, feel or smell,
imagined they were 'going down hill' or sickening for some
illness, never suspecting that there was any connection between
their wife's condition and their own.

Mrs. Chaplin died, if my memory does not err, around 1930,
and so visits to *The Firs* came to an end. With her death, my
wife and I had not only lost a dear personal friend, but we
feared that her passing would mean the severing of communication with Master K.H. Yet fortunately our fears proved to be
groundless, for only a short time elapsed before we met Brian
Ross, otherwise known by his books as David Anrias. B.R. had
spent some years in India and had acquired the ability to 'tune
in' to The Masters, in consequence another line of communication was established through him.

Not being comfortable in his rooms, he eventually came to
live with us as our guest for a time, and we found him to be a
most original and entertaining companion. He had known Dr.
Annie Besant, then President of The Theosophical Society, and

being a distinctly clever draughtsman had, while in India, drawn a number of cartoons for her, which had been published in one of the journals in which she was interested. Having associated with many theosophists, he was conversant with theosophical terminology and kept us much amused by a habit he had of introducing into everyday speech such polysyllabic terms as 'vehicles of consciousness', and other long words in which some theosophists delight. One of his waggish phrases was: 'I must now pull my vehicles together and get a move on.' Or he would say, with a most solemn face: 'World conditions are getting so dreadful, I really don't think I can hang on to my vehicle much longer.' He would refer to all persons as egos, and to stupid, conventional people as 'low-geared egos'. The bigoted members of the Society he called the 'rigids and tights', and those who seemed to imagine that 'pulling the long face' or indulging in 'the deep note' were signs of spirituality, he facetiously called 'gloomoids'. When bedtime came and he began to feel tired, he would get up from his chair and say: 'I am now going on to other planes', or 'I will now seek the horizontal'.

He could often remember his out-of-the-body experiences while asleep, and in consequence had many interesting things to relate, apart from those he 'sensed up' during waking hours.

While living under our roof he wrote *Through the Eyes of The Masters*,* to which I penned the Foreword. Although he had the power to 'tune in' to several of them, his own particular Master is he who is known by the name of Master Jupiter; the High Initiate, if I remember rightly, who specializes in matters of Science, and also Astrology; that much maligned and, alas, much prostituted science. Until I met Ross, my own attitude towards it had been the prevailing one of ignorant scepticism, but when I learnt that its real value did not lie in its alleged 'fortune-telling' aspects but in its ability to reveal character, physical and temperamental tendencies, I became a convert – though not a practitioner.

* Routledge.

I cannot be precise as to dates, but I do remember that some time during the 'thirties I suffered for a number of months from a condition nearly approaching a nervous breakdown. It occurred shortly after I had completed my book *An Outline of Modern Occultism*, at which I had worked long and strenuously. Brian Ross had warned me that if I were not careful I should get 'short-circuited', as he expressed it, and some years previously a palmist I met at a friend's house had predicted for me a 'bad patch' around the period concerned. Anyway, my indisposition took the form of abysmal depression, insomnia and a kind of exaggeration of the affections. B.R. 'sensed up' that I was going through a time of crisis, and it was a question for me alone to decide whether I would end my present incarnation or hang on for another spell. He said that Master K.H. could not intervene in the matter for the very reason that the choice had to be entirely my own. But however that may be, I have much to thank one of my ex-pupils, Margaret N., who took me in hand, so to say, and used all her ingenuity to distract my mind. I have also to thank the late Archibald Cockren, who gave me treatment during that difficult period.

Cockren was a remarkable man of high spiritual calibre. After much research and experiment he rediscovered the secret of alchemy and the transmutation of metals. He showed me, by the way, a few nuggets of gold he had made. I innocently said: 'If you can make gold, why don't you do so and put it to some good purpose?' But his answer was, first that he didn't want to, and secondly, that if he were to go and offer gold-nuggets to shops interested in buying them, he would have Scotland Yard personnel after him at once to know how he had come by them. 'Why, if some individual could produce that precious metal in any quantity, it would cheapen it and all sorts of complications would ensue,' so he maintained. Thus, he was merely concerned with making a 'gold elixir' to give to such of his patients for whom it was indicated. He had several of these elixirs, derived from various metals, one of which he prescribed for me, and with very beneficial results. I may add that he was an occultist of considerable knowledge, and a true altruist who was not interested in making money out of his treatments and remedies beyond the amount needed for his modest requirements.

On one occasion Cockren received a visit in the flesh from the Initiate who is known as The Hungarian Master. Although like the other Masters he is a great age, my friend told me that he looked about fifty. Among other things he told Cockren was that if human beings knew how to live rightly and had no more bad *karma* to work off, the normal span of life would be around two-hundred-and-fifty, after which time the first organs to deteriorate would be the kidneys. When the race is more highly evolved, people will no longer need to die of a disease, but will die of their own volition, having decided that they have lived long enough in one particular body.*

Cockren himself died soon after the end of the second world war. He had lived for others, never thinking to conserve his energies, and so, like Mrs. Chaplin, had worn himself out. Before he was taken ill he had said: 'I think my work is now finished.' Perhaps if he had not had this conviction he might have taken steps to cure himself. He was a delightful personality, what with the benevolence he radiated and his engaging chuckle, and truly might it be said of him that he was a saint, but without the odour of sanctity.

*This incident is mentioned in my book *An Outline of Modern Occultism*. (Routledge.).

CHAPTER XXXVIII

Musical Associates

THE late 'twenties and the 'thirties proved eventful for me as regards forming musical friendships. I met the New Zealand-born pianist Esther Fisher, and the Australian soprano Gertrude Johnson, both of them inspiring me to write certain of my more serious works. If it had not been for Esther Fisher – fine, sensitive artist that she is – I doubt whether I would ever have been moved to compose works for two pianos. As it was, we conceived the idea of forming a duo-pianist alliance, which ended in our getting a number of engagements at the B.B.C. One evening a week I would go to her flat, and after a recherché meal of her own cooking, we would practise at our repertoire, which included among other things *Variations on the Volga Boatsong*, by my late professor, Iwan Knorr. Although somewhat Brahmsian, I had always liked those Variations and wanted to pay a tribute to Knorr's memory by reviving them.

Having written my own *Variations for Two Pianos** on an original theme, I afterwards cursed myself for having made them unduly difficult, for it meant more practising as far as I was concerned than I altogether relished, the outcome being that Miss Fisher played her part better than I played mine. Indeed, I fear that my conscientious collaborator found me something of a trial at times; composers are apt to be slatternly virtuosi, though the eighty-six-year-old Baroness Rothschild of Frankfurt – an erstwhile pupil of Chopin – had once told me that I had a touch exactly like her master's! After all, a touch is not everything, even assuming the aged Baroness was not romancing. . . . My *Variations* evoked conflicting opinions, for whereas my publisher Robert Elkin, for one, was heard to

* Elkin & Co.

remark that the oftener he heard them the more they impressed him, some of the big-wigs at the B.B.C. disliked the work and did not wish to give it a further hearing. As against that, the late composer Benjamin Dale praised it highly, and remarked that I had found a new way of using *6ths*. He was a most waggish and engaging fellow. I recall him saying one night as he took leave of me after I had played him some of my latest efforts: 'Well, thank you for a delightful evening. It has warmed the cockles of my musical heart!'

The pleasant association with Esther Fisher resulted in my arranging several Bach pieces for two pianos. Among these were the well-known *Invention in F*, and the *Gigue in G* from one of his *French Suites;* both of which pieces I much extended and elaborated. For my friend Gertrude Johnson, the Australian soprano, I composed my Scena entitled *Rima's Call to the Birds*, after the fascinating story by Hudson. Basil Cameron included this Scena at a Festival of British Music he organised, at the suggestion of Percy Grainger, in Harrogate. Nevertheless it has had few, if any, performances since, despite some efforts on the part of the late eminent soprano, Dorothy Bond, to obtain a hearing of it at The Proms. Though I composed it some years ago, it is one of the works of mine I still happen to like.

I concertised to quite an extent with Gertrude Johnson, she singing my songs, with me at the piano. Finally she went back to Australia, where she was instrumental in forming a National Theatre and Opera-house which, I learn, has proved an unqualified success.

Around that time I also concertised with the distinguished cellist, Beatrice Harrison – whose poetic head always reminded me of a Botticelli painting. Many years previously I had spent a highly enjoyable three weeks with the Harrison family at Tremezzo, in the Italian Lakes. We stayed in a small *pension*, and I remember, what with the wonderful air and glorious scenery, I felt so exhilarated that the buxom proprietress used to say; 'Signor Scotti sempre allegro'. Beatrice was having a few finishing lessons with her eminent professor, Hugo Becker, who owned a villa on the lake-side in the vicinity. He was a smartly-dressed, pointed-bearded man, looking more like a diplomat than a musician, but unfortunately was not diplomat enough even to pretend to suffer gladly rising competitors for cellistic fame. Or was it only Casals, the mere mention of whose name caused him to explode into unrighteous indignation?

It was sometime during the 'thirties that Albert Coates conducted the Tone-Poem I then called *Disaster at Sea* in the Queen's Hall. Yet although Ernest Newman wrote that he found 'much to interest him' in the work, the other critics called it 'cinema music'; not, as one of them said to me, because they disliked the music itself, but because the temptation thus to describe it had been too great to resist! Incidentally, I soon afterwards lunched with Sir Thomas Beecham, who told me that a work by Berlioz he had recently conducted had likewise been labelled 'Cinema music', notwithstanding the fact, needless to add, that Berlioz had lived and died long before cinemas had even been dreamt of!

Apropos orchestral works, a good friend to me and my music during the thirties was the late Spanish-born conductor, Angel Grande, a musician of temperament and fine calibre. He produced my *Concerto for Harpsichord and Chamber Orchestra* at the Wigmore Hall, with Lucille Wallace as the harpsichordist. Somewhat to my surprise, the work evoked a favourable press, but even so has never been performed again. Grande introduced works of mine into Spain, and altogether championed my cause wherever and whenever feasible; indeed, if he liked a thing, his warm temperament was such that he liked it whole-heartedly and took it up with enthusiasm. As a conductor he had some curious mannerisms of a jerky nature, for as he waved his baton he seemed to be constantly shrugging first one shoulder then the other, as if he were doing some peculiar physical exercise.

I remember a somewhat amusing incident in connection with him. I was sitting with some other listeners in the ante-room of a large London drawing-room in which Grande was con-

ducting one of my works, when during an interval between the
items a discussion arose between a party of my co-listeners as
to whether the piece just performed was a recent or an early
work of mine. As none of them knew – why should they? – I
came to their rescue and remarked: 'I happen to know it *is* a
fairly recent work.' Thereupon they began talking among
themselves about my compositions. When the concert had
ended and we were gathered round the *buffet*, one of them
approached me while the others were standing by, and asked
what reason I had for supposing the piece was of recent date.
'I'll tell you a story,' I said, and I told him the incident of the
palmist, who after informing me that she saw (as she phrased it)
'such high inspiration marked in my hand', had entreated me
not to be led astray and try to 'imitate such hideous composers
as Cyril Scott and. . .' Here my companion interrupted with
some warmth and said: 'But I don't consider Cyril Scott *is* a
hideous composer'. . . . 'You haven't got the point of my story,'
I replied. 'I *am* Cyril Scott.' *Sensation!*

Angel Grande died a few years after the second world war
while still a relatively young man. Although I believe in taking
Art seriously, I think he took it more seriously than was good
for his health. Not long before his death he wrote to one of my
publishers asking them to let him have the first performance of
my *Ode Descantique* for String Orchestra. They replied in effect,
'with pleasure, provided the performance would be within a
few months'. This seemed reasonable enough, yet he was highly
indignant, and wrote to me saying, 'But that is preposterous'!

I have only possessed one other Spanish friend during my
life, and he also suffered from the taking of Art too seriously.
His name was Pedro Morales, and he was well known in London
musical circles as a somewhat eccentric and melancholy
individual albeit with a lovable nature. I was fond of Morales,
but it was very difficult to conduct a friendship with him, for he
would always turn up at any appointment or social engagement
at least an hour or two late. If one asked him to dinner at 7.30
he would arrive about 9 o'clock when the meal was entirely

spoilt and the domestics in despair. Having once arrived he would then stay till the early hours of the morning, by which time my wife was completely exhausted. He lived out at Chiswick, and must have spent a fortune in taxi fares to get home after all other means of transport had ceased for the night. How he came to live there was as strange as the man himself; he had gone to dine with some people there for the first time, and had stayed, not for a few hours, but for over thirty years! Towards the end of his life he became more and more melancholy and so intractable that a kind friend had finally taken steps to ship him back to relatives in Spain, where he died during the 'thirties. My memory of him is flavoured with both affection and some gratitude, for he was a good critic of a constructive kind. Being a violinist, though he did not play professionally, he was very helpful to me while I was at work on my *Violin Concerto*, parts of which I altered at his suggestion.

Another friend I remember with warm affection was Bertram Binyon, a cousin of Laurence Binyon the poet. Binnie, as his associates called him, was a singer of the more refined *lieder* type, and a most engaging and original personality. He was half English and half Italian, which may have accounted for some of his lovable characteristics. In his latter years he had become very stout and grown somewhat to resemble Queen Victoria. Everybody who had the good fortune to know him loved Binnie, and in his company no one could feel dull for a moment. He was a most entertaining raconteur, partly because curious things used to happen to him, the most curious of all being an experience he had had as a young man when embarking on his career as a singer.

He had been engaged to sing at the Crystal Palace, under the conductorship of August Manns, long since deceased. He was in the middle of his performance when he noticed with some surprise that the people at the back of the huge audience began to rise. Soon more and more rose and started surging towards the platform until the whole place was in a state of confusion. Then a huge elephant, in a rage, appeared through one of the back entrances, and after trampling down the chairs as if they were so much matchwood, finally made its exit through one of the large side-doors, followed by its agitated keepers. The irony for my unfortunate friend was that he had hoped for great things from his appearance at such important concerts. But not at all. When the notices appeared in the paper, his name was not even mentioned, the whole write-up being devoted to the 'hero' of the occasion – the infuriated elephant.

For some years Binnie being a popular figure in London society, gave recitals and did a certain amount of teaching. His English was not always quite idiomatic, which only added to his charms. Sometimes he was not always fortunate in the choice of his accompanists. 'Why don't you get So and So?' I suggested on one occasion. 'Ah,' he replied, 'these swell accompanists are no use to me. They won't come to one's flat to rehearse, so one doesn't get the chance to –er– feel one another till one gets on to the platform.'. . . I was often together with him at house-parties, where he always livened up everything with his contagious laugh and humorous remarks. In middle life he got married, retired to the country, and being a very versatile man devoted himself to painting. He eventually went to live at Dulverton, and as for a time I was staying not far distant at Exford, I was able to see him quite frequently. He was then nearly seventy, and, alas, had contracted a complaint for which the doctors urged an operation. I pointed out that there were less drastic and less dangerous treatments for his trouble – but all to no purpose. He allowed himself to be operated on, and subsequently died, to be missed by all his many friends.

I cannot conclude this chapter on friendships without mentioning the only society woman I have ever genuinely loved. At the time of her death I was at work on my *String Quartet II*, and to express my sorrowful feelings I included an *In Memoriam* movement in that opus. Yet when I say that I loved Ena Mathias, otherwise Mrs. Robert Mathias, I do not mean that I was in any sense *in* love with her, but that I felt for her the warmest platonic affection of which my nature is capable. As a personality she was almost unique, and her hospitality and kindness of heart were well-nigh limitless. She was a tall, statuesque woman, with a persuasive inflection and way of speaking which were quite irresistible. An ardent devotee of music and the fine arts, to her lavish table came musicians, artists and other notabilities.

Some of my happiest recollections are of week-ends spent in her company and that of her large family at her country house in Sussex. She possessed among her other endearing attributes a prodigious sense of humour, which sometimes showed itself in curious ways. When we were alone together in the garden, she would incite me to talk about matters occult – in which she did not believe – and then when I came out with one of my 'fantastic' statements, would go off into fits of good-natured laughter as if the whole thing were a stupendous joke. This of course only incited me to pile it on all the thicker. Nevertheless, and here is something which may interest spiritualists, my 'extravagant' discourses were destined in the end to have unexpected results. It so happened that around the time of her death I was often together with one of my clairvoyant associates, a Miss L—, who without any difficulty got into *rapport* with my departed friend. Miss L— was not a trance-medium, but possessed the natural faculty of seeing and hearing disembodied entities. She had never met Ena Mathias and knew nothing about her, and the only means of first establishing *rapport* was through a letter which I had kept. But after the prime contact had been made, Ena used to appear every time I had a 'sitting' with my clairvoyant acquaintance, who would repeat to me all that she clairaudiently heard. Incidentally, she commented on Ena's 'pretty way of speaking', as she expressed it.

One of the first things Ena told us was that, although she had laughed at my occult 'revelations', they had sunk in all the same and had made a lot of difference to her now that she had passed over: they had, in fact, helped to orientate her in her new though happy surroundings.

I am not writing these *Memoirs* to convince sceptics of the truth of personal survival – people usually believe what they *wish* to believe or to disbelieve – nonetheless I may mention something which might be regarded as of an evidential nature. Although I had never noticed the trinket concerned, she told us that she used to wear a cameo surrounded by some filigree ornamentation. She said it was not of much value, but that she had especially liked it, and was anxious that I should have it as a memento. Out of interest, I subsequently asked one of her sons if this information was correct, and the answer was, yes, she had possessed such a cameo. Needless to say, I did not ask him to give it to me, for, apart from other considerations, I need no trinket to remind me of a friend I am unlikely to forget.

CHAPTER XXXIX

Break-Up of Family Life and Subsequent Events

WHEN in 1939 the second world war eventuated, it broke up our home for good. My children, who were still relatively small, had to be got out of London at almost a moment's notice, but as my married sister owned a little house in Somerset, she was able to accommodate both them and myself. As for my wife, she was able to share a domicile near Rye with our mutual friend, occultist and gifted writer, A.K. Challoner, with whom she stayed till the end of hostilities.

We now realised how fortunate it was that my son had been born some three years *after* my daughter, Vivien, for otherwise he would have been of military age and hence forced to risk his life in the fight against Hitler. As things turned out he was just old enough to join the Navy when the fighting was practically over, went on a long cruise which enabled him to see the world, and so, as my devout mother was wont to remark, all was for the best.

With regard to myself, I spent the whole of the war years in the West Country in rooms, guest-houses and hotels, and having no piano, and conditions being unfavourable for composing, I devoted myself entirely to literary work.

According to Brian Ross, I was for some two years in the early 'forties under 'the most atrocious astrological aspects'. He told me, pulling a long face, that they were the worst ones it was possible to have. 'Oh well,' I said, 'after all, two years is not very long in a life-time.' 'My *dear* Cyril,' he rejoined, 'believe me you will *never* survive them.'. . . I remember that after hearing this discouraging news I walked straight into a hunchback. That means, I thought to myself, that my friend's pessimistic forecast may not be so serious as he imagines. Which is not to say I believe that unfortunate hunchbacks, piebald horses etc., can actually *bring* one good luck, they are simply omens, and therein lies the difference.

As for my 'atrocious aspects', not only have I survived them, but I did not even notice them to any great extent. What devotees of astrology so often fail to realise is that it is not the aspects in themselves which greatly matter, but how one reacts to them. Granted that the break-up of one's home-life might be to numerous people a dreadful calamity, the more so if, as in my case, they were unable to carry on with their work or profession – one reads how Chopin suffered in Majorca while deprived of his piano – but as I had other work and absorbing interests, it made all the difference. Indeed, had I not been chagrined by the tormenting thought that hundreds of innocent folk were slaughtering each other or being bombed to bits, my war years would have been on the whole relatively enjoyable.

The first year, after leaving my sister's house (my children having gone to their respective boarding-schools) I spent in rooms at Barnstaple with my old friend and fellow student, Holland-Smith, with whom I had always remained in touch. He was now getting frail, and suffered considerably from depression and some other ailments of an intractable nature for which he received palliatives from one of the doctors. But, as the depression persisted, I finally induced him to try a homoeopathic remedy, in which he had no belief; and that, vulgarly stated, did the trick. He had always displayed a sceptical and somewhat disapproving attitude towards my unorthodox medical opinions, and was not entirely pleased that he should in the end have been helped by unorthodox means. In any case he thought it rather *infra dig* and time-wasting that I, a musician, should write therapeutical books at variance with conventional ideas on diet and the like. As for my philosophico-occult ideas, he absorbed many of them, but I think rather regretted that I had committed them to paper.

We left Barnstaple together in '41 and stayed at a guest-house in that delightful but ill-starred Devonshire spot,

H

Lynmouth. Incidentally, one day he was taking a walk when he met an acquaintance, to whom he remarked: 'I have got my old friend Cyril Scott as one of my fellow-guests. Of course you know his name?' . . . 'Let me see,' she said pensively. 'Ah, yes. He's a composer of light music and pretty songs, isn't he?' Evidently by then the erstwhile musical *enfant terrible* had become quite polite and harmlessly insignificant! And yet, immodestly though gratefully to say, this opinion, it would seem was not held by one of my colleagues. For staying at the same guest-house was the composer and organ-virtuoso, Frederic Curzon: we used to play enjoyable games of chess together. During our joint stay, the B.B.C. gave a performance of my *Pianoforte Trio*, before which the announcer had rather implied, or so Curzon thought, that whilst I was best known as a writer of small pieces – 'best known' was quite true – I sometimes tried my hand at bigger works. This apparent slight on my abilities so incensed the generous-minded Curzon that, as Holland-Smith told me, he had come down from his room in a high state of indignation.

Around that time I was more than ever pestered by a lot of correspondents as the indirect result of my books on Occultism. Indeed, I should be at some pains to count the number of letters received from women asking me to put them in touch with a Master, or failing that, act as guru to them myself. One woman, who first called on me uninvited, subsequently suggested by letter that I should not only be her spiritual Teacher, but should be her lover as well! Needless to say, I could only inform all these good ladies that I was merely a humble server, and hence quite incompetent to accede to their flattering requests; therefore all I could do was to remind them of the occult adage: 'When the pupil is ready the Master is forthcoming'.

Yet whereas these importunate souls were easily dealt with, less so others. One of them was a voluble pen-wielder of the fairer sex who sent me piles of manuscript with the entreaty that I should give out her occult revelations to the world. The scripts used to arrive every day despite my protest that what she asked was quite beyond my power to do. Another woman – though this was before the war – urged me to proclaim that she was a reincarnation of Madame Blavatsky, who, judging from her general make up, she quite obviously was not. Other women sent me trivial and illiterate verses of a spiritistic nature, requesting me to set them to music and induce the B.B.C. to perform them. Some curious requests also came from America. One man wrote asking me to make the most fantastic assertions about sex for inclusion in one of his own scripts.

But the strangest entreaty came from a young American singer, now deceased, who during the 'thirties had come to England to be coached by me in the rendering of my songs. From this unfortunate girl I received during the war dozens of mad letters, telling me I was her twin soul, and begging me to fly over to the States and give recitals with her, after which as the result, so she said, Peace would surely be declared!!

After living at Lynmouth for some twelve months I decided to transfer myself to a hotel at Exford, one of the picturesque little villages on the Somersetshire moors. Although I knew no one there, as it subsequently turned out, the move was to form a link in a chain of events which, from the occult angle, was to prove of considerable importance for me. But of that later.

I liked Exford, save for one thing; it is a stag-hunting centre, and I loathe the cruel sport of hunting, and find the conversation of hunting people unspeakably boring whenever obliged to listen to it. Whatever may be said to the contrary, the fact remains that the curious pastime of chasing and killing animals for pleasure is a relic of barbarism, and I venture to predict that when the human race is more evolved, hunting will vanish with some of our other barbarities.

During my stay in the village, my *Ode to Famous Men*, for Tenor and Orchestra was performed by the B.B.C., but the then manageress of the hotel evidently did not think it or me of sufficient importance to warrant her lending me her private sitting-room wherein to hear the work in quietude. In consequence I had to listen to it in the bar, to the accompaniment of clinking glasses and noisy chatter. But on another occasion, when a programme of my songs and some violin pieces was performed I was more fortunate, for the bar happened to be empty save for one elderly woman who was interested enough to be present, and who afterwards remarked: 'I do love your songs – they are so dainty.' (!)

I had been in Exford for many months, and was sitting alone in the *salon* one evening in early spring, when in walked a soldier, with whom I got into conversation. Speaking of Barnstaple, he told me that he had recently lunched with some friends at a very pleasantly situated guest-house named Broomhill, a few miles from that town. 'When you get tired of this place,' he said, 'you may like to sample it' – and he proceeded to give me more particulars. Little did I then imagine to what developments this apparently chance meeting was going to lead. And yet, as I later on came to know, there was no chance involved; it was an available means used to a given end. Anyhow, I went to see Broomhill, stayed a few weeks, and was so charmed with the place that I resolved to return there, and unless anything unforeseen happened, remain for the duration of the war.

Broomhill, which lies in a charming valley, is a place which especially appealed to my country-loving heart, with its picturesque garden, its surrounding hills, woods and burbling stream. But apart from these rural attractions and the congenial people I contacted there, its great significance for me lies in the fact that at Broomhill I first made contact with the soul who was destined to become my present link with Master K.H., communications with whom had been severed for some years . . .Marjorie H., who does not wish to be mentioned more specifically in these pages, had made a disastrous marriage at an early age, which had resulted in her husband finally deserting her after she had endured a number of years of conjugal unhappiness. Further, shortly before I met her, she had lost, through death, a great friend, a bereavement which was all the more poignant because at that time she was an agnostic, though not a fanatical one, and therefore had no belief in any form of survival.

By the time I met Marjorie, I had long since learnt that it is both futile and in bad taste to thrust one's own beliefs on other people. After all, it is one thing to write books about Occultism, which the reader can accept or reject, but quite another verbally to bore people with such matters when, because of politeness, they cannot just tell one to shut up! Nevertheless, if I encounter a soul to whom esoteric philosophies might bring some consolation, I do not forget the deeper significance of the text, 'Blessed are they that mourn, for they shall be comforted', – that is to say, comforted, not through sentimental sympathy, but through the acquisition of Knowledge and Understanding.

That Marjorie, at that time, was such a soul, I correctly surmised, for no sooner did I tentatively approach the subject of Occultism than she reacted favourably at once and was eager to hear everything I could impart. Indeed, it seemed evident that she had known it all before and that I was merely re-awakening a knowledge, which for *karmic* reasons had been temporarily cut off in her present incarnation. This often happens in the case of souls who are faring along the Occult Path; for it is needful that, through a period of suffering in a given life, certain *karma* should be worked off before the Master can be consciously contacted, or before nescience can be supplanted by knowledge. Sometimes a prolonged illness has to be endured, so that, as Master K.H. pointed out, through the weakness of the body the higher consciousness may be released, and such an illness Marjorie did have to suffer while I was staying at Broomhill. It was, in fact, during that illness that Master K.H. first appeared to her. Although I had often spoken to her about The Masters and had shown her the original of the drawings of them which appeared in David Anrias' book *Through the Eyes of The Masters*, she had never imagined for a moment that she would ever see one of them, at least during her life-time. And therefore what happened was entirely unexpected.

She had been fast asleep, when gradually she became conscious of a very strong light. Thinking she had perhaps dozed off and left the electric light on, she opened her eyes, and there, standing near the foot of the bed was the tall figure of Master Koot Hoomi, and it was the radiance of his aura which had wakened her up.

'Why, it's Master K.H.!' she exclaimed. Whereupon he smiled and slightly bowed in assent.

'You are getting better,' he said.

'And for that I have to thank C.S. . ,' she replied.

'*We* know he is looking after you,' he said with a twinkle, putting a finger on his lips: and she knew what *that* meant, for though she was in the hands of the doctor, I had been giving her some biochemic remedies. (They do not clash with orthodox treatment.) Then the light he radiated began to dazzle her, and she had to close her eyes. When she opened them again he had gone.

The incident, devoid of all ceremoniousness, had only lasted a few minutes. Would she think in the morning that it had merely been a dream? To ensure against that possibility, she switched on the electric light, got a pencil and paper and made a note of the happening.

Master K.H. at that time visited her two nights in succession, and I think it was to impress on her that he was a reality and no vision which could be conjured up by the imagination. But whatever may have been his intention, since that year '44, when, incidentally, I was sixty-five, he has appeared many times to give guidance or suggestions relative to the work, and even to the more mundane matter, indirectly connected with it, as to where one should live in the difficult period when the housing problem was so acute. . . And here ends the story of how in unforeseen ways, communication was once again re-established with my Master.

CHAPTER XL

New Work for Me and New Abodes

WHEN the war was nearing its end, my wife became worried as to what was to happen to me. Before the war we had lived in a large house, with adequate domestic help to look after us, and with our respective work-rooms sufficiently far from each other for me to pound on my piano without disturbing her too much while she was writing her novels. But the war had changed everything; a large house with several domestics was no longer a feasible proposition; besides which, my wife's poor health was such that she felt she could no longer cope with it. In view of all this, she contrived to snap up a small domicile in London, whilst Marjorie, who was homeless, agreed, in accordance with K.H.'s wishes and intentions, to be a companion to me and look after me when and where we succeeded in finding a suitable home. This arrangement not only relieved my wife's anxieties but those of Marjorie's widowed mother, who lived at the other side of the world, and with whom I had corresponded. As I had now reached the autumnal age when it is sometimes possible to act as 'guide, philosopher and friend' to a soul who might find that trinity acceptable, I wrote to her saying that I would be honoured to regard her daughter as, so to say, my unofficial ward; though at the time I refrained from mentioning that had it not been for the kind offices of an Indian Mahatma I might never have met her daughter at all!

Having reached the age of sixty-five, I had decided that it was best to give up the idea of composing any more, and if not to rest on my laurels, for I had none to rest upon, at any rate to devote my energies to other possible forms of usefulness. It had become obvious that my more serious compositions were not wanted by the musical powers that be, and it seemed futile to write works unlikely ever to get a hearing, considering the large number I had already composed which had not been granted even a single performance. I had some forty years ago indirectly helped to extricate British music from the academic rut in which it had got fixed, and having performed that office, it might well be that *that* was all I was destined to do along musical lines in this particular incarnation!

However, the Fates, or rather the Masters decided otherwise, and my resolve to turn my back on music came to naught. For while we were still at Broomhill, K.H. appeared to Marjorie in his wonted manner, and told her that *they* had new work – music-work – for me, and that in the circumstances it would be advisable to accept an invitation to stay with a certain lady, a fellow-devotee of Occultism, who had rented a large house in Devon near the coast. This lady, having read my books, had written to me more than once during the war years, suggesting that we should do some work together, but as I then knew practically nothing about her and was engaged in other activities, I had not reacted to her proposal. Nevertheless, when K.H. intimated that he now wished us to make the contact – Marjorie was included in the invitation – we bid a somewhat sad goodbye to Broomhill, and set out for our new destination, with confidence but also with some curiosity. The visit, he had said, would at least be 'a stepping stone' to other destinations.

The new work he had in mind for me was my third Opera, which I have called *Maureen O'Mara*, and much of the libretto of which I had written before the second war. The subject is an Irish one of my own creation, the turn of Irish phrases having appealed to me as a most suitable language for musical setting. In fact the libretto almost wrote itself, if the extravagance be pardoned. I embarked on the new operatic work while Marjorie and I were staying, with the lady I will refer to as Mrs. X after we had left Broomhill.

I hold the theory, shared by Ernest Newman, that it is best, when possible, for a composer to be his own librettist; that is, of course, provided he has the essential dramatic and poetic instincts. The truth is that when it comes to the actual composing, so much of the libretto has to be altered, bits of it lengthened, bits of it shortened and so on to create the right balance, that all sorts of annoyances may arise if *two* persons are engaged on one and the same work. Apart from other considerations, librettists are apt to be touchy and resent it if the composer takes liberties with perhaps those very portions they have 'written with their heart's-blood'. I will not go so far as to say that unless a man can write his own libretto he had better at all costs confine himself to other types of music, but I do say that composers incapable of so doing are apt maybe for that very reason to choose very ineffective opera or even oratorio texts, as witness those of Delius, Hindemith and others.

We had hoped to remain with Mrs. X for several months, but before half that time had passed, she had some trouble with her landlord, and announced one day, as if she had sensed it clairvoyantly, that we should be leaving on such and such a date. I fear, if the truth be told, that her clairvoyance sometimes got a good deal mixed up with her own personal inclinations, and although she was undoubtedly imbued with the spirit of service and was gifted with healing powers, some of the entities with whom she was or thought herself in touch had apparently an accommodating habit of saying at times the very things she would have wished them to say. In any case, having in this delicate manner been given notice to quit at the very time when I was in the throes of my new work, we should have found ourselves in a serious quandary had I not received an unexpected note from my old friend Percy Grainger, in which he offered us the loan of a small house his wife possessed in Pevensey Bay on the Sussex coast.

And yet, although this would have solved our immediate problem, it would also have meant living too far, as I thought, from London's musical activities. However, thanks again to our Friend and Guide K.H. who one breezy night appeared in the french-windows of Marjorie's bedroom – he had to restrain the

H*

flapping curtains with his hands while he spoke – my doubts about accepting Grainger's offer were liquidated.

The outcome was that we lived in Pevensey Bay for some two and a half years, during which I finished the actual composing of my Opera, though I did not orchestrate it. . . . In connection with which I am reminded of the implication that I was a better librettist than a composer. For when the 1951 Festival of Britain was pending, I sent the piano score to the Arts Council *after*, in accordance with the ruling, first having submitted the libretto. But whilst the worthy members of the committee approved of and accepted the libretto, they rejected the Opera itself. Not that its rejection either greatly surprised or depressed me, seeing that there is in the make-up of creative artists something that tends to cause them to lose interest in previous creations as soon as they start on new ones; and this I had already done. Still, as The Masters had originally expressed the wish that the Opera should be written, I was sorry on *their* account for what had happened in the end. There was also the question as to whether I should spend long months orchestrating the rejected Opera or just set it aside for good and all. But fortunately to decide me came a message to the effect that although they (The Masters) had *hoped* that the Festival might have provided an opportunity for the work to be produced, they had not underestimated the powerful forces which would be used against it by those who were not working *with* them. Meanwhile, in the circumstances, it would be advisable to concentrate on work which could be more readily performed.

While living in Pevensey Bay, it happened that after completing some shorter works, I suddenly had the urge to write a non-sectarian Oratorio, otherwise a universalist choral work, which I thought to call *Hymn of Unity*. But being uncertain whether my urge could be 'trusted', I did not actually engage on it till I had received the assurance that the undertaking was approved of; whereafter I wrote the libretto in about three weeks and finished the whole work in around six months. Not that I hoped for a performance of it in the near future, since I fully realised that until the Aquarian Age – the Age of unification we have just entered – had got more under way, it might be asking too much of any British choral society to produce an English Oratorio which embraced other religions besides the Christian. Thus I do not expect my *Hymn of Unity* will be either performed or published during my life-time.

Having come to the end of our sojourn in Pevensey Bay because the Graingers needed their house for some relations, we should have again been homeless had we not made the acquaintance of a gifted astrologer, Madge Gladwin (not all good astrologers are necessarily men) whose parents owned a little flat on their small estate among the Downs near Eastbourne, in which they said we could live if so minded. Naturally the offer, coming at such a timely moment, was gratefully accepted, and confidently so, seeing that K.H. had manifested to tell us that the change was in the interest of several aspects of The Masters' work.

Our years in Pevensey Bay had been happy, busy, and I venture to hope, useful ones. The atmosphere of the Graingers' house had been conducive both to the writing of the bigger works and to those shorter and less elaborate ones which could more readily be performed; whilst at the same time Marjorie's psychic and intuitional faculties had so much increased that she acquired the ability to hear Master K.H.'s voice 'as clear as a bell' whenever he wished to communicate without actually materialising. Likewise her ability to remember her out-of-the-body experiences had increased, as also to see the *astral bodies* of persons who had recently passed over and desired to convey some message.

After we had settled in the little flat, we had many enlightening talks with our new astrologer-friend Madge Gladwin, who explained for me, from the astrological angle a matter which had often puzzled me relative to the frustrations I had experienced. Why, I questioned, should The Masters, who know all about the influence of the stars, bother to use me, or any other other receptive composer, for the creation of some lengthy musical work at a time when the prospects for its performance were not at all favourable, or were even definitely bad? And the reasonable answer I received was; that although the astrological aspects at a given time might be excellent for the inspiring and composing of a particular kind of music, it by no means follows that they must also be good for its getting a hearing. From The Masters' point of view the first thing is to get the work written; the rest if needs be can wait – sometimes even as long as till after the composer's death.

And on this astrological note I will end this chapter.

CHAPTER XLI

My 7oth Birthday: Clash of Opinions

O NE never likes to land anybody in an embarrassing situation,
yet such was my fate when at a party given in honour of
my seventieth birthday, Sir Steuart Wilson, then Music
Director of the B.B.C., was good enough to face the delicate
ordeal of paying tribute to the honoured guest. Being among
the notabilities who consider me 'a back number', his speech
was a masterpiece of eloquent evasion. Ingeniously avoiding
any allusion to my work or merit as a composer, with con-
summate skill he contrived to convey the impression that he
was saying nice things about me, when actually he believed
there was little nice, musically, that *could* be said. As evidence
of this, a letter was later dispatched from the B.B.C. to one of
my chief publishers, stating in effect that whilst it was conceded
that I could write *salon*-pieces and songs of a pleasing character,
my would-be more serious efforts were not the type of music
that organisation wished to further. Although, it went on to
say, the B.B.C. had been happy to honour my seventieth
birthday by giving performances of two of my larger works
(both of them, I may here interpolate, having been written
thirty to forty years ago) they nonetheless could not be regarded
as artistic successes.

Meanwhile, as an amusing example of how opinions may
differ, I had received messages and letters from several
distinguished musicians, among them a particularly generous
one from John Ireland, all of them telling me in so many words
that, although the said works might have been written so long
ago, the dust of Time had failed to tarnish their freshness!
Further, the German music-journal *Melos* had seen fit to honour
my birthday with a portrait-embellished article, in which among

223

other things it was stated that I was one of the few English composers whose works had achieved world-recognition! As against that, however, Mr. Hugh Ottaway, writing in *Musical Opinion*, declared that I was a composer who had had the misfortune to outlive his reputation and his 'message'; the inference being that it might have been better for me, and perhaps for others, if I had managed to die at an earlier date! This article, nevertheless, aroused the ire of certain musicians, one of them being Mr. Montagu Cleeve, who countered with an indignant protest, contending that it was most unfair to pass judgment on any composer unless familiar with his latest and more representative works. (One cannot be familiar with unheard works or unpublished manuscripts!)

It was all quite entertaining, especially as round the same time I received an irate letter from a woman, who having heard a broadcast of my little *Hourglass Suite*, upbraided me for my 'hideous nerve-racking discords' and charged me 'never to write such music again'! As the complaint lodged against me by my detractors is seemingly that I am not discordant enough, this letter was distinctly encouraging.

The other side of the medal, if less amusing, was more encouraging still.

While the B.B.C. was voting against my worthiness to be considered a serious composer, I received out of the blue a letter from war-shattered Berlin respecting one of the very works – *Piano Trio I* – which the B.B.C. had ruled was 'of little musical interest'. The letter came from Frl. Olga Metzeltin of the *Metzeltin Trio Ensemble*, and informed me that she and her colleagues had performed the work many times with tremendous success, and regarded it as one of the outstanding contributions to the trio-literature of the world! Incidentally, I have received several letters from her since, in which she asks for more of my works, and, with that marked German respect for personalities, insists on addressing me as 'Dear and highly esteemed Master'!, the envelopes, despite my protests, being addressed to *Sir* Cyril Scott – a distinction to which I have never aspired.

Around my seventieth birthday other news came from Germany. After an interval of some years, my German publisher, Herr Willi Strecker, head of B. Schotts Söhne, Mainz, paid a visit to London. Without any mention of the subject by me, he suddenly said: 'I am simply amazed at the way you have been neglected in England. In no other country could such a thing happen.' He then told me that in Germany whenever the subject of British composers cropped up, my name still held an honoured place. Moreover, I heard soon afterwards, much to my surprise, that Richard Strauss had referred to me 'in very gratifying terms'.

Meanwhile, from the Continent had come a letter from the eminent French composer, Florent Schmitt, its object being to effect a meeting between the Hungarian violinist, Dr. Francois D'Albert and myself. This meeting produced unforeseeable results; for apart from being a musician with outstanding gifts, D'Albert turned out to be such an ardent admirer of my works that he organised an entire concert of them in Dublin, where he lived for a time after choosing to leave Hungary for political reasons.

At his request, I went over with Marjorie to Ireland for the concert, and at the same time gave a talk over the Radio Eireann. Whether I deserved the reception I was accorded both by the musical notabilities and the press is not for me to say. Anyhow, it was cordial in the extreme, and I was hailed as 'a grand old man of English music.' As for the generous-hearted D'Albert – who, incidentally, insisted on calling me 'Master', rather to my embarrassment – he told me that while touring the Continent he had met many 'friends of my music'.

The honour paid to me in Dublin was soon to be followed by a somewhat similar one in London. In the Autumn of 1951 *The Music Teachers' Association* gave a concert consisting mostly of works of mine which had *not* been written thirty or forty years ago, and for which D'Albert came over to play my then recently composed *Sonata Melodica*. (A year or so later, by the way, the eminent violinist Max Rostal proposed to the B.B.C. that he should broadcast that work, but his proposal was declined). Speeches were made by my publisher, Mr. Robert Elkin, and by Dr. H. Lowery, author of *The Background of Music*, who generously referred to me not only as a composer of serious music but also as a writer who had influenced his own outlook and that of many others.

CHAPTER XLII

Conclusion – 1959

I have now just passed my 80th birthday – and looking back along the long road of my life, I consider I have arrived at the most satisfactory and contented stage of my journey. To be free of those harassing, embarrassing and turbulent emotions which start with childhood and continue long into manhood, I regard as a blessing. I also regard as a blessing that freedom from those distractions so hindering to creative work. Age having brought that 'divine indifference' prized by some philosophers, I still obey the urge to write music, but without worrying at all about the prospects of its performance. And yet this confession should not for a moment be taken to suggest a lack of gratitude to those who, believing in me, have exerted and still exert themselves to get my works performed. I also owe a debt of gratitude to those musical *littérateurs* who in the music journals and even in some dailies have paid warm tributes to me and at the same time have fulminated against what they regard as my neglect, about which Professor Norman Demuth had gone so far as to write: 'A prophet is often unhonoured in his own country, but the complete neglect of Scott is something inexplicable'. Not that I myself see it in quite that light, for if I may venture to say so, rather have I been misrepresented than neglected. (After all, might not this be said of any composer whose very minor items were often broadcast, yet some major work only every five years to mark his birthday? However –)

Events during the last ten years included two visits to Dublin – I love the Irish and their delightful turns of phrase – where the ever enthusiastic Francois D'Albert had organised two more concerts of my works. Not long afterwards he sailed for Canada, to our regret but to his advantage, and in some ways to mine;

for he is not one to keep his enthusiasms to himself, but somehow contrives to make them contagious. Indeed, being a really fine artist, his word carries weight. After a few years in Montreal, from which town he did some extensive concertising, he has now become President of *The Chicago Conservatory of Music* – an important position to hold, and one, so he writes, which has already enabled him to arrange a concert of my more representative compositions.

Among other events, I wish gratefully to mention that the distinguished musician, Dr. Vernon Griffiths, of the University of Canterbury, New Zealand, organized a 'Cyril Scott Festival' of four concerts in 1958. And it was gratifying to see from the programmes he afterwards sent me, that Dr. Griffiths does not regard me as merely a composer of 'pleasing *salon* pieces and songs', for among the items chosen were several of my most representative works both for piano solo and two pianos. . . . I also wish gratefully to mention my meeting with Sir Thomas Armstrong, who at the time had recently become Principal of the R.A.M. In this broad-minded musician and lovable man, I was to find a generous friend of my music. In fact, he told me that he would do all in his power to further my works. Somewhat prior to my 80th birthday, he wrote an article for the *Musical Times*, headed 'Cyril Scott; A Pioneer' (recalling the days long ago when perhaps I might have been thus called). Moreover, nearer the date of my anniversary he lent the concert hall of the R.A.M. for the party given by my publishers, Mr. Robert and Mr. William Elkin to mark the occasion: at which he made a speech the gist of which cannot modestly be repeated here.

Finally, importantly and also gratefully, I would mention the B.B.C. Although the music journals criticized it for not including one of my orchestral works in the 1959 'Proms', it honoured me in other ways. My erstwhile pupil, since become the eminent composer, Dr. Edmund Rubbra, broadcast a most charming and touching tribute to me, whilst Professor Demuth gave a discourse illustrated by fragments selected from the most representative of my early works up to one of my very latest, the 3rd Piano Sonata. (Esther Fisher, in /58 had broadcast this work in its entirety, but despite many requests for a repetition, the B.B.C. had done nothing about it. Further relative to my 8oth birthday, a recital of my songs figured in The Home Service, yet as they were all more or less early period efforts and one or two mere potboilers, I hardly think that even with Mr. Bryan Drake's fine singing they could have enhanced my reputation!

In America my birthday did not pass unnoticed, since from New York came news of a lengthy broadcast interview with Percy Grainger, who being my oldest living friend was credited with knowing as much about me and my music as could be known! He has since died, much to my loss in this world. Also, from Holland came news of a broadcast of my prize-winning *Piano Quintet.* . . . But at the risk of boring the reader, I have already said more than enough. Nevertheless, it would be ungracious of me not to add that The International Academy – World Fraternity of Scholars recently made me both an Hon. Mus.Doc. and a Fellow of this estimable Fraternity.

These last few pages of my book I am writing in a house I have bought among the Sussex Downs. Away from noise, and with its high, pure air and the charming view to be seen from its windows, it is ideally suited for any composer to pursue his vocation. What had happened was this; one day I suddenly felt the inclination to visit some friends who had just moved into a new house. And I was so taken with its situation and outlook, that they said: 'Why not buy the house that's for sale next door?' But though I was inquisitive enough to go and peep through its uncurtained windows, I did not feel the least tempted to acquire the property. However, the night following, Master K.H. materialized to tell us that they (The Masters) had pointed the way to a new environment, where they hoped with my co-operation to create their chosen centre for inspirational work with far-reaching effects. This was the exact message, and I make no comments. And yet when it came to carrying it out, there were many annoyances and setbacks. Marjorie was not only very reluctant to leave the flat we had lived in for seven years, but when she first saw the house concerned she took an intense dislike to it, and tried to persuade herself and me that it was not the one Master K.H. had really meant. However, in the end all doubts were dispelled, for when after a lot of delay and trouble with builders and decorators we had finally moved in, he appeared once again, this time to express his thanks and to give us and the house his blessing. . . . Since then, Marjorie has come to love the house, whilst my wife, and such friends who visit us congratulate us on our good luck in having found 'such a delightful abode'! And here we continue to live happily with no less than four siamese cats!

I can presently write finis to this book and leave it to its fate. But whatever that may be, I consider it would not have been worth writing if merely concerned with the vicissitudes of a British composer, and if all the incidents of an occult nature had been suppressed. Apart from the fact that without mention of them, these *Confessions* would have been incomplete, my object in relating them was not to draw any special attention to myself, but to The Hierarchy and The Masters. Indeed, far from supposing that I in particular have been singled out to be used by, or as they modestly put it, to work *with* them, I would stress that numerous others are likewise working with them, be it in connection with the fine arts or other activities pertaining to the emancipation of mankind. But as most of these men of goodwill, not excluding women, are unaware whence some of their ideas or inspirations come, if endeavour were combined with that knowledge, a closer *rapport* could be established. And that is one reason why, now that religious intolerance and religious persecution are no longer such a formidable obstacle, The Hierarchy wishes to come more into the open.

CHAPTER XLIII

Afterword – 1969

THERE comes a time in one's life when one is apt to think that nothing more worthy of note is likely to happen again, albeit where my own life is concerned this cannot be rightly said. For since I thought to write finis to these memoirs, several things of significance have occurred; the most significant having been the formation of a Cyril Scott Society with the object of promoting performances and recordings of my major works. The idea of forming such a Society, which had never been envisaged by me, was first conceived by the distinguished musician, Dr. W.R. Pasfield, and this aroused the interest of a number of other distinguished musicians including notably Sir Thomas Armstrong, the then Principal of the Royal Academy of Music with the gratifying result that the initial concert of the Society, thanks to Sir Thomas, was able to be given in the Duke's Hall of the R.A.M. Featured in the programme were such eminent artists as John Ogden, Peter Pears accompanied by the composer Edmund Rubbra, whilst The Alberni String Quartet gave a most excellent performance of my String Quartet No. 2 (published 1955). The concert was very well attended, and in every respect a pronounced success.

But this was not the only concert exclusively devoted to my works; there were others, namely in Ireland, which were brought about by the accomplished Hungarian Violinist, Francois D'Albert, who after the war had emigrated to that country, where he had lived for several years prior to settling in U.S.A. and there becoming one of the head professors at the Chicago Conservatory of Music, which later through D'Albert's influence conferred on me an Hon.Mus.Doc. of that scholastic Institute – that kind of degree, I may mention, *en passant*, never having been accorded me in my own country.

Alluding to men of repute, Nietzsche wrote in *Thus Spake Zarathustra* 'Some die too young and some die too old. The precept sounds strange. But die at the right time!'

Yet whether it would have enhanced my musical reputation if I myself could somehow have contrived to carry out that injunction, and so in my case to have died young, is a matter of conflicting opinion, as these autobiographical confessions may have served to show. And yet to confess my personal opinion, however far-fetched it may seem to non-occultists; for me to have died young in this particular life-span would have meant my not living long enough to experience the vicissitudes of a ripe old age – that experience being desirable for the furtherance of my spiritual evolution.

Also, living long has enabled me late in life to receive a number of letters from music-lovers abroad, generously telling me how always the writers have enjoyed my music; some of them adding how favourably it contrasts with the cacophony which during the last few decades has become a fashion. There is, however, an occult explanation regarding this fashion which I wish to mention. According to the Initiates, there have existed for a long time certain evil thought-forms which could alone be dissolved by means of discord and in no other way. Hence was the ultra-discordant phase of music put through to effect that purpose; though it was never intended it should be more than a transient phase.

And at that I will leave it to the consideration of the reader, and will end my book on this informative note, and with my grateful thanks to all those friends of my music and myself who have supported the various measures to bring about its furtherance.

Appendix I

The following are the actual tenets of Occultism:

That there is no such thing as the supernatural, but only the supernormal; that Spirit is Matter in its rarest aspect and Matter is Spirit in its, to varying degrees, grossest form.

That both humans and animals survive death, the higher domestic animals possessing evolving, reincarnating souls, the lower species what is termed a group-soul.

That there is a Hierarchy of High Initiates who seek to further the spiritual evolution of the backward, contentious humanity on this planet by inspiring the *best* in philosophical, religious, scientific, ideological and artistic trends. But as Man has a measure of free-will, They only seek to *guide* and never to coerce.

That these Initiates can in certain circumstances be contacted by those in whom the spirit of service to humanity is developed.

That regarded from the occult viewpoint, the basic truths of all the great religions are the same – it is only in their exoteric expositions that they differ.

That the Higher Occultism rightly embraces the twin doctrines of Reincarnation and *Karma*, the latter being the law of cause and effect carried to its logical conclusion.

Occultism, being the synthesis of Philosophy, Religion and Science, is in disagreement only with some of the scientists' still unproven assertions and negations.

Appendix II

For the benefit of the interested reader, the following brief data about some of The Masters is appended.

The supposition that all The Masters live in Tibet is erroneous. Those few who live in that country are known respectively under the names of Master Koot Hoomi (K.H. for short), Master Morya, Master Djwal Khul (D.K. for short) and the very High Initiate called the Bodhissattva Whom we in the West call The Christ. K.H. is of Kashmiri origin, was Pythagoras in one of His previous incarnations, and among His other activities has much to do with music. He is well over a hundred-and-fifty years of age, is over six feet tall, has a fair complexion, hair and beard of a golden brown, and eyes of a wonderful blue. He speaks English perfectly. Master M. is a Rajput Prince, and Master D.K. is a Tibetan, and when writing through His amanuensis Mrs. A. A. Bailey, calls himself simply 'The Tibetan'. The Bodhissatva, known as The World-Teacher occupies a Celtic body, and lives not far from the other Masters in Shigatse.

There is a Master living in or associated with all the larger countries of the world. He Who is known as Master Jesus lives in Syria and occupies a Syrian body. He travels much in European countries. There is a Hungarian Master named Count Rakoczi Who has a residence in the Carpathians, and He also travels much, notably in South American countries. There are two English Masters, but where They live may not be revealed. I believe I am correct in saying that in all there are about two hundred Masters, but only a comparatively few of Them have pupils, for Their time is taken up with other Work in the service of humanity.

Appendix III

According to Occultism and those who are in a position to *know*, the catch-argument that all proof of an after-life is lacking because 'no dead person has ever returned to tell us about it' is partly based on ignorance as to what constitutes our complex human make-up. The idea that a man is just a body with a vague thing called a soul hidden somewhere inside it, or else floating above it attached to a sort of string like a child's balloon, is entirely at variance with the truth as known to those who can *see*. Factually, a human being while living on earth consists of a physical body *plus* several interpenetrating subtler *bodies* (these constitute the aura) or 'vehicles of consciousness' composed of much finer matter and higher vibratory rates. Without these *bodies* there would be no consciousness in the physical body at all. Indeed, instead of the latter being the actual engenderer of consciousness, it tends to act as a damper on it; *therefore* when death comes and the individual is released from the necessity of having to function through that body, far from relapsing into a state of tranquil slumber, (the 'rest in peace' idea) he finds himself very much more alive than when in his cumbersome 'garment' he was treading the earth-plane. Strictly speaking, there is only one difference between sleep and death; after sleep the individual comes back to his fleshly body in the morning, whilst after death there is no body to come back to! With practice, some people can learn to remember their out-of-body experiences at night, for it is largely a question of training the brain to register more subtle impressions than normally it does at present. But we learn from The Masters – who can function in any of their subtler bodies at will – that when the race is more evolved, the memory

235

of experiences on the higher Planes during sleep will no longer
be cut off. Moreover, in the comparatively near future an
increasing number of persons will be normally and sufficiently
clairvoyant to see so-termed spirits, i.e. disembodied entities,
and then the whole attitude towards misnamed death will be
changed for ever. (In parenthesis I would point out that the
word 'higher' as applied to Planes is inaccurate and merely
used for convenience; for the word really means a higher rate
of vibration, the Planes being interpenetrative.)

Appendix IV

The ordinary dominant 7th. chord (1.3.5.7.) which now I never use.

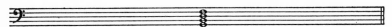

The basic chord (1.4.7.) I most frequently use, on any degree of the chromatic scale.

The chord as used both in similar and contrary motion.

etc.

(from *Theme and Variations for Two Pianos.*)

The chord employable as a sustained bass.

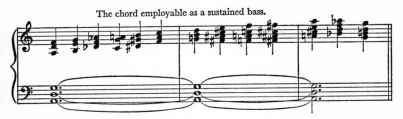

Appendix V

Judging from the important part that melody (or melodic phrase) has played in the past, it is most improbable that it will play no role in the future. Instructive to note is that melodies that have stood the test of Time are simple and, easily discernible. It is the *treatment* of them which reveals the master musician.

Theme of the magnificent Chorus I, *St. Matthew's Passion.* Bach.

Violin Concerto. Beethoven.

Tristan and Isolda. Wagner.

String Quartet. Ravel.

Index